Sensible Sensuality

A Collection of Essays
on
Sexuality, Femininity and Literature

Sensible Sensuality

A Collection of Essays on Sexuality, Femininity and Literature

Sarojini Sahoo

AUTHORSPRESS
Publishers of Scholarly Books

Worldwide Circulation through Authorspress Global Network
First Published 2010
by
Authorspress
E-35/103, Jawahar Park
Laxmi Nagar, Delhi-110 092
e-mail: authorspress@yahoo.com

Sensible Sensuality: A Collection of Essays on Sexuality, Femininity and Literature
ISBN 978-81-7273-541-8

Printed in India at Tarun Offset, Delhi.

Dedicated to

My Friend, Professor K.V. Dominic

Preface

A prime figure and trendsetter of feminism in contemporary Indian literature, Dr. Sarojini Sahoo has written extensively about the interior lives of women and how their burgeoning sexuality is seen as a threat to traditional patriarchal societies. Her works treat women as sexual beings and probe culturally sensitive topics such as rape, abortion and menopause from a female perspective. For her, feminism is not a gender problem or confrontational attack on male hegemony and, as such, differs from the traditional feminist views. Writing with a heightened awareness of femininity, she has developed an appropriate style that exploits openness, fragmentation, and non-linearity.

Dr. Sahoo accepts feminism as a total entity of femalehood which is completely separate from the man's world. She refutes the limits that patriarchy places on female sexual expression and identifies women's sexual liberation as the real motive behind the women's movement. Although writing on sexuality of women and advocating women's rights give her great satisfaction, Dr. Sahoo refuses to be restricted by labels. She explicates, "I think it's more important to be a complete human being than a writer or a feminist. But I also realise the reciprocal nature of living and writing. I believe that living gives you material for writing while writing helps you to interpret your existence in a meaningful way. I live, I write, I grow."

This publication is a collection of prose by Dr. Sahoo, in which she paints the difference of sensibility towards sexuality between male and female and has her own credibility for the frankness to deal with sensitive matters. She explores why sexuality plays a major role in our understanding of feminism. "I write on these topics to begin a discussion on female sexuality and help bring about change," says Dr. Sahoo, who is admired for breaking sexual and cultural taboos through her writing. It is hoped that the readers will gain a better sensibility of sensuality after reading this book.

Sudarshan Kcherry

Contents

1 Bicycle and Me

I am the second daughter of my parents. Before my birth, my father was expecting a son and when I was born, he was not present beside my mom. Finding me a female baby, my mother had a shock, because my birth might be the reason of her humiliation in future. She told me later, she could not sleep the night with fear of facing my father with a girl child. She was praying all night to God for changing my gender, but God did not pay attention to her pathetic cry and hence my gender was not changed. But my father was a strong-headed man and he could not forget his sorrow of not becoming a son's father. He wanted to bring me up as a boy. My hairstyle was made in such a way that whenever my father would look at me, he would have the idea of being a proud father of a boy. I was dressed in boy's shirt and pants. Father even called me with a boyish name: LALA.

When I was a child, we were residing in a semi-joint family. The brothers of my father had their own families, who had divided their ancestor's properties but still living together with separate kitchens. I had a group of cousins of similar age and ironically all were boys. With them I had to play boyish games like sword fight game, shopkeeper and customer game, even gullidanda and thief-police game. I had not played with dolls, neither had I worshiped the Goddess Khudurkuni or the God moon on Kumara Purnima day or as a girl child does in Orissa. I belonged to a business family. My father owned a rice mill (still it exists). He engaged himself as a commissioning agent. So in our house there were four to five bicycles for the use of the manager and workers of the mill. Father's bicycle was the tallest and the most handsome one. I was attracted by its appearance. Nobody dared to touch the cycle. My cousins were expert in bicycle riding and I could not control my instinct to ride thc same one.

Once on a hot summer midday, while my father was having his aiternoon siesta, I took the cycle and took it through the narrow lane behind our house (our house was facing the main road). There I attempted half-pedal riding. This lesson, though a risky one, continued for a few days and once I was caught by a relative redhanded. But in spite of scolding me, he encouraged me and taught me how to ride a bicycle. He held the back of the cycle and assured me not to worry about the balance. Very confidently I rode the cycle. But after a while, when I looked back, I found the well wisher standing a few metres away from my cycle. Suddenly I lost my balance and fell down. But that incidence gave me courage to ride the bicycle on half pedal. It all happened when I was a student of class V. Later I was able to move on the full pedal. But as my father's cycle was very high, I felt inconvenient to ride on it.

I had a cousin, who was residing in a village. He was very short in height and so was his cycle. He used to visit our house at frequent intervals. When he paid a visit, I was the first beneficiary, as I had an opportunity to ride his short cycle, which was most convenient for me.

Later I was provided with a gent's cycle by my father. But this time also no new bicycle was purchased for me and I had to be content with the old one. So, I can't say what the cost of my bicycle was at that time.

My bicycle riding was a sort of freedom to me, and I used to make a tour from Korian to Govindpur (the two corners of Dhenkanal town) every day. I had the experience at roaming on the vacant road of the town at hot midday, to pick up mangoes from the tree by standing on my bicycle.

Once, a complaint was made to my father that I was competing against a running lorry truck with my bicycle.

But my riding was also a great help to all the relatives and neighbours as I was often asked to buy vegetables or grocery from the market. I had become a convenient mode of communication for my elders to exchange their notes and messages with their classmates. All these were possible due to my bicycle.

I had a friend, Rajiv Mishra, in class VII. I used to take him to the school on my bicycle. He used to sit on the rod of the bicycle and I had practised to ride double. Unfortunately he committed suicide. I really felt lonely as I had to go alone on my cycle.

Once I was rewarded by one of my elder cousins for my efficiency in bicycle riding. We were going to our village on the bicycle. It was a few kilometres away from the town. On the way we had to ride on an elevated road. My cousin proposed a contest for me. He told if I could ride the cycle on the elevated road, he would give me a box of chocolate and finally I won the box.

I enjoyed the freedom of riding that bicycle up to class IX and after that I had to say goodbye to it because my guardians thought I was too old for my tomboy activities.

Did any boy pass a remark on my cycling? I didn't care for any remarks, but once a naughty boy tried to intercept me and when I got down from my cycle, he quickly allowed me to move forward. As far I remember, very few girls rode cycles at that time. Though the Govt. College of Dhenkanal was far away from the town, I had no opportunity to ride it again in my college life as the State Road Transport Authority was providing the college bus regularly. But, nowadays times have changed and I find my girl students usually come to college on their bicycles. Whenever I wrote any story regarding my nostalgia, the bicycle figured in it there. Some of the stories related with my bicycle experience are *Parajita Samrat*, *Udibar Bela* (*Time to Fly*), *Moho Bhanga* (*The End of fascination*), etc.

Hearing my tomboy experiences of adolescence, one of my Portuguese philosopher friends once asked whether this had any impact on my sexuality in later life. Such questions could not be asked in India, because here any query about sexuality cannot be shared publicly and moreover it is an offence to ask any lady such a question. Whatever Judith Butler may say, it is true that my 'tomboy activities' had no impact in my later life. Regarding sexuality I am straight, though you may find the gayness in one of my stories '*Nepathye*'. Later it was included in my English story collection[1] as "Behind the Scene". In my adolescence, though I wore boyish dresses, yet whenever I was sent to the mill by my father for supervision of work in his absence, a strange shaky and shy feeling gripped me, because the workers looked at me with curiosity and their eyes expressed a lot. It seemed that they were looking for a girl under a boyish disguise and the girlhood inside me felt abused. Perhaps, a girl was always living in me under the boyish garment. But our society is not so smart as to discuss these things.

Sexuality is something that can be related to a lot of other aspects of culture, tightly woven into an individual life, or into the evolution of a culture. Anyone's class or ethnic or geographic identity can be closely tied to his/her sexuality, or anyone's sense of art or literature. Sexuality is not just an entity in itself. But still, either in the West or in the East, there is a reluctant outlook towards sexuality, and society has always tried to hide it from any open forum. The censorship on speech, adding decorum to dress, and declaring the sexual organs as subjects, society has imposed a ban on it. However, in spite of such self-imposed censorship, sexuality has its place in public forum; in religious and spiritual texts to establish any philosophical notion; judiciary and legislative documents;

medical textbooks to *explore* the human body and lastly literature.

But neither society nor the legislative, nor the judiciaries advocate or propagate sexuality. In the West, James Joyce's *Ulysses*[2] or Radclyffe Hall's *The Well of Lonliness*[3] or Virginia Woolf's *Orlando*[4] are some examples which have invited criticisms for describing sexuality in literature. In the West, sexuality in literature grew with feminism. Simone De Beauvoir in her book *The Second Sex*[5], elaborately described the gender role and problems due to biological differences. Later Judith Butler explored the gender problem in a queer theory and the total West experienced a new 'third sex'; the genre came into existence.[6] It does not mean that there was no sexuality in literature previously. The literature of every corner of the world has its sexual affixation, but those were not in form of any movement or did not base on any manifestation.

In Indian literature, like the West, sexuality comes with the growth of feminism but unlike the West, very few has been written on trans-sexual experiences. The sexuality still exists in the heterosexual form as it was in the past. But the voice has changed a lot. No doubt, sexuality in current literature is different from the erotic descriptions of the text we found in the last centuries.

Cathy Nelson, a student of Orleans University, was preparing her project on feminism and asked me if I felt that feminism in India was different from feminism in the West. If so, how?

I answered her with the example of ancient Vedic India where we find that there were equal rights of man and woman, and there were even feminist law makers like Gargi, Madalasa and Maitreyi, but I think India in later Vedic period had grown into a polar dichotomy society of male and female, where the former oppressed the latter and treated them as the 'other' or similar to the lower caste. Patriarchy is just one of the hierarchies, where females are most oppressed as in the traditional system. In India, arranged marriages are always preferred, and love marriages are considered as a matter of social sin and shame. Many Indians contend that arranged marriages are more successful than marriages in the West, particularly given the latter's staggering divorce rates. Romantic love does not necessarily lead to a good marriage, and often fails once the passion dissipates and real love flows from a properly arranged union between two individuals, they argue. An unmarried daughter—pronounced a spinster even in her late twenties—brings shame upon her parents, and is a burden. But once married, she is considered the property of her in-laws.

In this context unwed mothers, separated, single, or unfaithful women are considered outcasts. Living out of wedlock with a partner is still virtually unheard of. During her marriage, the bride's father has to pay dowries in the form of money, furniture, jewellery, expensive household items and even houses, or arrange expensive foreign holidays to the bridegroom. The phrase "bride burning" was coined in India after several young brides had their saris lit on fire in front of a gas stove either by their husbands or in-laws because of their fathers' failure to meet the demands for a bigger dowry. As a custom and tradition of a joint family, a bride has to face her tyrannical in-laws and still traditional Hindu society rejects divorcees. In the case of sexuality, the active role of a woman has always been denied—a woman should not be open to sexual desires. You may find many women who have crossed their menopausal stage without having a single orgasm in any day. In religious rituals and customs also females are barred to take part in all worships. In Kerala, females are not allowed to enter in the Aiyappa temples. They are also barred from worshipping God Hanuman and in some regions they are not allowed even to touch the 'linga' idol of Lord Shiva.

In recent politics also though all political parties have assured to reserve thirty three per cent of seats in legislation in their manifesto, still it has not been transformed into law as the male-dominant political parties are opposing the bill. In financial matters, though women are allowed to work outside, yet their rights on any household matters have always been denied. A woman has to work in the kitchen, even if she is an earning member, and also go outside for her job. The husband will not take charge of the kitchen, though he remains unemployed, as a man cooking for the family is considered to be against his manhood. Legally though, according to the Court, sons and daughters have equal rights on patriarchal property but still as per practice, ownership changes hands from father to son and the role of a daughter or a daughter-in-law is ignored.

My long answer to Cathy Nelson was sufficient to make her wonder how male hegemony still exists in the Oriental countries. Since that day I have been planning to write this essay on feminism for the Western readers. Two queries always worry me: whether the term 'feminism', always defined with respect to the socio-economic scenario of Europe, America and the rest of world is meaningless, and the second one is most important for me as it is always a query in my mind whether it is essential at all for the West.

The first wave feminist Mary Wollstonecraft's thoughts on the *Education of Daughters* or *A Vindication of the Rights of Woman* seem to be more practical in context with Asia and Africa, though I know my colleagues of the third wave feminism in Europe may laugh at my comments. It is undoubtedly true that before Simone De Beauvoir's *The Second Sex*, the sexed body was not an object of phenomenological investigation. Beauvoir changed that. Its argument for sexual equality works in two directions. First, it exposes the ways in which patriarchy exploits the sexual difference to create systems of inequality, and exposes the facts of sexual politics, which later leads to feminism to fight against male hegemony. She also claimed that so long as the standard of equality is the male body, the discriminatory sexual difference remains in play. Second, her book acts as a prime source for the gender theories developed by Judith Butler or others in a later period. But what about her novels and short stories? Simone's few short stories and her novel *The Blood of Others*[7] are an attempt to establish a right to abortion, and her first novel S*he Came to Stay*[8] provides a fictional portrait of her unconventional relationship with her lifelong partner, Sartre, and her protégé, Bianca Bienenfeld. "Mandarin" is a love story examining the complex dilemmas posed by love and marriage (i.e., existential relationships are easier in theory than in reality) on fictionalised account of Beauvoir's passionate affair with Algren. Her *Memoirs of a Dutiful Daughter*[9] offers an intimate picture of growing up in a bourgeois French family, rebelling as an adolescent against the conventional expectations of her class, and striking out on her own with an intellectual and existential ambition exceedingly rare in a young woman in the 1920s. In my opinion sexuality is more prominent in the writings of Erica Jong and Germaine Greer, if we consider them as writers of a later period.

Erica Jong's novel *Fear of Flying*[10] or Germaine Greer's novel *The Female Eunuch*[11] were two prominent books which dealt with sexual desire of women. Greer once told the *New York Times* in 1971, "Women have somehow been separated from their libido, from their faculty of desire, from their sexuality. They've become suspicious about it. Like beasts, for example, who are castrated in farming in order to serve their master's ulterior motives—to be fattened or made docile—women have been cut off from their capacity for action. It's a process that sacrifices vigour for delicacy and succulence, and one that's got to be changed."

I admit, sexual liberty is a major question for third-wave feminist in Europe, and it is an important question, but for the Asian African feminist, still the questions once raised by Mary Wollstonecraft have their own importance. I think, the essentiality of feminism always adhered to the liberation of the women of the world, not of only women of Europe or America. So, when Erica Jong's protagonist tells: "my nipples stand up and salute the inside of my bra (or in this case, dress—since I'm not wearing a bra)..." it becomes meaningless for the women of Asian and African countries, because for them, not wearing the bra is not a question of revolt, rather it is against their social custom.

Wearing or not wearing a bra may not refer to sexual orientation but to sexual behaviour. A sexual orientation is different from sexual behaviour because it refers to feelings and to self-identity rather than only actions. Persons may or may not express their sexual orientation in their behaviours. Sexual orientation refers to emotional, romantic, sexual attraction, infatuation from one person to another person or persons. Someone's sexual orientation is categorised according to the gender(s) or biological sex of the people he/she has these feelings for, that is, it describes whether a person is attracted primarily toward people of the same or the opposite sex, or to both. Sexual orientation exists along a scale that ranges from exclusive homosexuality to exclusive heterosexuality, and includes various forms of bisexuality. Sexual orientation is an important part of a person's total self-identity: how we see ourselves and how others see us. A person's experience and understanding of her/his sexual orientation can vary during his/her life.

You may have certainly marked that most of our world-famous writers from Flaubert to Sartre are at their most creative when trying to get a date—for better or worse. So sexual behaviour is the core element of humans' sexual nature, but not sexual orientation It does not mean that sexual orientation has no role in creativity. In other words, sex is often the spark behind creativity; even if you're not having sex. For instance, you can look at the erotic sculptures of the Konark or Khajuraho temples or you can access the *Shringar Kavyas* of

"Riti Yuga" in Indian literature. They are more of the sexual behaviour of an artist than his sexual orientation. The same kind of art can be found in Western countries also. It's harmless enough if you can show it in temples, children can view it in the art museum, or even on a computer with "safe search" turned on. But there's no denying that there's a sexual behaviour behind it. They are the artistic expressions by an artist where a woman has her clothes off. There's a sexual element every time an artist depicts the human body, naked or not.

Human bodies are shaped by sex, and not just the sex organs. Muscles, hair, skin, posture, everything about us is shaped to a degree by our sexual behaviour. So every painter or photographer is in some way engaging his/her sexual behaviour when he depicts a human being. And not just in visual arts, but also in drama, literature, music, dance, sports, every form of art. Art that depicts humans, depicts sexuality. The same thing can be found in Western art.

In Botticelli's Venus or Georgia O'Keefe's flower paintings, or Henry Dreyfuss's styling of steam locomotives for the New York Central, we find either sexual behaviour present in explicit form or in implicit form. Shakespeare filled his plays with sexual double entendres and allusions. In every play he finds ten ways to make a joke on the word "coxcomb". In his day the word "nothing" was slang for female sex organs, so the title *Much Ado about Nothing*, takes on a second meaning in a play about virginity and trust. At other times the sexual behaviour is virtually hidden. Take the last movement of Beethoven's fifth symphony. The rhythm has an unmistakable sexual energy. And the modulation, up to a fifth, when the theme is repeated, feels sexually rooted also. Or take Piet Mondrian's paintings. There's no explicitly sexual reference in most of them. Yet I sense a strong sexual impulse behind them. I imagine him painting in the same mood you might have while making love, with the same intensity, creativity, and the desire to really connect. Well, you might disagree about Piet Mondrian. Thus at is kind of obvious to say that sexual behaviour is a huge element in art. I think that's a good thing. The world would be a lot poorer without sexual energy in art, music, literature, drama, architecture, design, poetry, cooking, and even in religion and spiritualism.

Generally in Greco-Semitic family, God is described in masculine terms. But in the Indic family, we find God is considered as both masculine and feminine form. In Taoism, *Yin* and *Yang*, and in Hinduism *Prakriti* and *Purusha,* are considered feminine and masculine. The concept of *Ardhanarishwar* form of Lord Shiva in Hinduism is also considered as the major factor of gender equality, and for this in ancient India we find evidence of homosexuality, bisexuality, androgyny, multiple sex partners and open representation of sexual pleasures in artworks like the Konark and Khajuraho temples, being accepted within prevalent social frameworks.

In Samkhya philosophy, The concept of *Prakriti* and *Purusha* in Samkhya Philosophy was later accepted in buddhism and the *Bhagavad Gita.* We may define *Prakriti* as 'female' or negative charge and *Purusha* as 'male' or positive charge. *Prakriti* is all-pervasive but a complex primal substance, which is transformed into multifarious nature. The primal entity is not perceived in its original form, for then it is in a state of equilibrium, and as such remains non-modified. This eternal and infinite principle is insentient, and consists of three interdependent and interchangeable elements called the *gunas.* These are *sattva, rajas* and *tamas.* These *gunas* are not the qualities but the constituent parts of Prakriti. They give complexity to *Mula* (original) *Prakriti.* But *Purusha* is inactive and passive, but sentient and also infinite and eternal. Under the inscrutable influence of *Purusha*, the equilibrium in *Prakriti* is disturbed, and the whole universe of unlimited permutations and combinations comes into existence. The first modification of *Prakriti* - primordial nature - is called as *Mahat* or Cosmic

Intelligence. It further involutes into two forces, (1) *Akasha*, the primal matter, and (2) *Prana*, the primal energy. *Akasha* forms the material basis, and *Prana* the energy basis of creation. From the interaction between *Akasha* and *Prana* are formed five subtle elements, crudely translated as Ether, Fire, Air, Water and Earth. In various proportions, these are the constituents of all the material existence in the universe. As can be seen, even *Mahat* or Intelligence is matter consisting of three *gunas*, and five elements.

In physics also we find that an atom is made up of protons and electron. A proton is a positive charged particle and an electron is negatively charged particle. The attraction between the proton and the electron made the existence of an atom possible.

Later, this concept led to the Shiva and Shakti dual theory of creation. Adi Shankaracharya, the founder of non-dualistic philosophy (Advaita—'not two') in Hindu thought says in his *Saundaryalaairi*—"Shivah Shaktayaa yukto yadi bhavati shaktah prabhavitum na che devum devona khalu kushalah spanditam api", i.e., It is only when Shiva is united with Shakti that He acquires the capability of becoming the Lord of the Universe. In the absence of Shakti, He is not even able to stir.

In *Brihadaranyakopanishad*, it is stated that the genesis started from the sexual intercourse of the Creator and a cow. The cow was running from the Creator with the fear of being raped and 'she' was transforming 'herself' into different forms, but the Creator found 'her' every time; from the sexual intercourse (or we may describe it as a 'rape') the genesis started. I don't find any reason why we the Indian people get so worried about Wendy Doniger.[11] I do admit that the Western thinkers portray Hinduism inappropriately through Greco-Semitic concepts and categories. I often find my Western philosophers examine *Bhagavad Gita* as a negative term of Arjuna killing his relatives because of his Hindu outlook. But as Hindus, we are also very much sensitive to an issue like sexuality, especially when it is related with our religion and spiritualism. But we have to admit that sexuality is often described in our myths, *Puranas* and in our religious texts, above all in our literatures from medieval age to this post-modern age.

But in India, nowadays most of the people mingle sexuality with passion and physical co-adherence, and to some extent to perversion with a hidden concept of sin in their puritan mind. Actually the term 'sexuality' has a wider aspect. Sexuality involves not only passion and perversion but also biological or physiological sex, gender, gender identity, gender roles and sexual orientation. The growing trend of feminism has now compelled the intellectual brains to think twice about the definition and role of sexuality in Indian society.

Notes and References

1. Sahoo, Sarojini, *Waiting for Manna* (Short Stories Collection). Vadodara: Indian AGE Communication, 2008.
2. Joyce, James, *Ulysses*, Penguin Books, 1992.
3. Hall, Radclyffe, *The Well of Loneliness*, Knopf Doubleday Publishing Group. (reprint publication 1990).
4. Woolf, Virginia, *Orlando: A Biography*, Ed. Rachel Bowlby, Oxford University Press, 1998.
5. Beauvoir, Simone de, *The Second Sex, 1949*, Trans. H. M. Parshley, Penguin, 1972.
6. Butler, Judith, "Performative Acts and Gender Constitution: An Essay in Phenomenology and Feminist Theory", *Performing Feminisms: Feminist Critical Theory and Theatre*, Ed. Sue-Ellen Case, Baltimore: Johns Hopkins UP, 1990.
7. Beauvoir, Simone de, *The Blood of Others*. Pantheon, 1st Pantheon pbk. ed edition, 1984
8. Beauvoir, Simone de, *She Came to Stay*, W. W. Norton & Co. 1999.
9. Beauvoir, Simone de, *Memoirs of a Dutiful Daughter*, Harper & Row. 2005.
10. Jong, Erica, *Fear of Flying*, Holt, Rinehart and Winston, Austin, Texas, 1973 (1st edition), and Greer, Germaine, *The Female Eunuch*. Mcgraw-Hill. First Edition. states edition, 1971.

11. Wendy Doniger (born November 20, 1940) is an American scholar of the history of religions. Much of her work has focused on translating, interpreting and comparing narratives and myths of Hinduism. She is often criticised for her negative portrayals of Hinduism. The book *Invading the Sa-cred: An Analysis of Hinduism Studies in America*, (Edited by Aditi Banerjee, Antonio De Nicolas and Krishnan Ramaswamy and contributed by the scholars like anthropologist Prof SN Balagangadhara, religion scholar Prof. Arvind Sharma, noted psychologist Dr Alan Roland, and educationist Dr Yvette Rosser and published by Rupa & Co, Kolkata demonstrates how the lack of vigilence and indigenous expertise has enabled a small group of Western scholars like Wendy Doniger to usurp and assume the Hindu authoritative voice and to use it for defaming, demonising, distorting and eroticising the Hindu/India image through Freudian psychoanalysis; and how technology like the Internet facilitated the mobilisation of Diasporic voices against this trend in American academia.

2 A Feministic View on Sexuality

It is an interesting fact that any concept before occupying any philosophical frame, came to literature first. Gender problem was discussed in Virginia Woolf's *Orlando*[1] and Radclyff Hall's *The Well of Loneliness*[2], much before Judith Butler.[3] Sexuality was also acceptable in literature in Joyce's *Ulysses* or Thomas Hardy's novel. Before writing *The Second Sex*, Simone's two fictions *She Came to Stay* and *The Blood of Others* were published, where a reader can find the topics somehow related to sexuality. But it is undoubtedly true that before *The Second Sex*, the sexed body was not an object of phenomenological investigation. Simone changed that. Her argument for sexual equality works in two directions. First, it exposes the ways in which patriarchy exploits the sexual difference to create systems of inequality and exposes the facts of sexual politics, which later leads to feminism to fight against male hegemony. She also claimed that so long as the standard of equality is the male body, the discriminatory sexual difference remains in play. Second, her book acts as a prime source for the gender theories developed by Judith Butler or others in a later period.

I think regarding sexuality, Simone seems to be most prominent in her essays, especially in *The Second Sex* or in *Coming Age* than in her novels. Her few short stories and her novel *The Blood of Others* are an attempt to establish a right to abortion and her first novel *She Came to Stay* provides a fictional portrait of her unconventional relationship with her lifelong partner, Sartre, and her protégé, Bianca Bienenfeld. "Mandarin" is a love story examining the complex dilemmas posed by love and marriage (i.e., existential relationships are easier in theory than in reality) on fictionalised account of Simone's passionate affair with Algren. Her *Memoirs of a Dutiful Daughter* offers an intimate picture of growing up in a bourgeois French family, rebelling as an adolescent against the conventional expectations of her class, and striking out on her own with an intellectual and existential ambition exceedingly rare in a young woman in the 1920s. In my opinion sexuality is more prominent in the writings of Erica Jong and Germaine Greer, if we consider them as writers of a later period.

I always want to paint sexuality opposed to Indian patriarchy concept, where women's sexuality is used for raising of children only and there is no seat for their sexual desire. In my novel *Upanibesh* (The Colony) I have taken the symbol of "Shiva Linga" as the sexual desire of women. Medha, the protagonist of *Upanibesh*, was a bohemian. In her pre-marital stage, she considered it boring to live with a man life-long. Perhaps she wanted a free life, where there would be only love, only sex and no monotony. In my various stories I have painted lesbian sex, rape, abortion, infertility, failed marriage and menopause. I have been criticised for using the word 'fuck' in my story "Rape".

I can say only in the Oriental perspective. I think, sexuality has a major role in understanding feminism. Let us consider a girl's condition in the adolescent period. If she becomes pregnant, the male partner is not blamed for his role. It is the girl who has to suffer. If she accepts the child, she has to suffer a lot socially and if she goes for any abortion, she has to suffer emotionally for the rest of her life. In the case of married woman, there are many restrictions with respect to sexuality whereas her male partner is free from these restrictions. Even now in Oriental countries, you can find most of the married women ignorant about their feelings of orgasm. If a female admits about her sexual pleasure, there may be every chance of her being misunderstand as a bad woman by her own husband. She may be misunderstood for having pre-marital sex. At the time of menopause, except for some biological changes, nothing has changed in sexual life, but a woman has to suffer a lot mentally, thinking herself unfit for satisfying her husband sexually. I think till now in Asian and African countries, the patriarchy society has its control over sexuality. So, the women need two types of liberation. One is from financial slavery and another from sexuality. Women are always victims; men are oppressors. I believe in the theory: "a woman's body, a woman's right", which means women should control their own bodies and people should take them seriously.

References

1. *Orlando: A Biography*, published in 1928, was not Woolf's most famous work, but it was one of her most intense considerations of gender. Through the life of the extraordinary character Orlando, Woolf examines the meanings of masculinity and femininity as these definitions changed in Europe over the course of four hundred years. In tracing those changes, Woolf presents a feminist overview of history from the days of Elizabeth the First to the end of World War I. Orlando, who was modelled on Woolf's close friend Vita Sackville-West, goes from being a young man in Queen Elizabeth's court to a love affair with a Muscovite princess; from Ambassador Extraordinary to encounters, now as Lady Orlando, with the famous English writers Pope, Addison and Swift; finally, Orlando experiences childbirth. Woolf, Virginia: *Orlando: A Biography*, edited by Rachel Bowlby, published by Oxford University Press, 1998.
2. *The Well of Loneliness*: Originally published in 1928, Radclyffe Hall's this novel is the timeless story of a lesbian couple's struggle to be accepted by "polite" society. Shockingly candid for its time, this novel was the very first to condemn homophobic society for its unfair treatment of gays and lesbians. The book has three things a modern reader has to get over: archaic theories of sexuality, purple passages and novel expectations. The theory can be marvelled at as

a museum piece. The purple passages can be appreciated as period literary stuff. Hall, Radclyffe: *The Well of Loneliness*, Knopf Doubleday Publishing Group, reprint publication 1990.

3. In her most influential book *Gender Trouble: Feminism* and the *Subversion of Identity* (1990), Judith Butler argued that feminism had made a mistake by trying to assert that "women" were a group with common characteristics and interests. That approach, Butler said, performed "an unwitting regulation and reification of gender relations"—reinforcing a binary view of gender relations in which human beings are divided into two clear-cut groups: women and men. Butler notes that feminists rejected the idea that biology is destiny, but then developed an account of patriarchal culture which assumed that masculine and feminine genders would inevitably be built, by culture, upon 'male' and 'female' bodies, making the same destiny just as inescapable. That argument allows no room for choice, difference or resistance. Butler thus offers what she herself calls "a more radical use of the doctrine of constitution that takes the social agent as an object rather than the subject of constitutive acts." Butler, Judith. "Performative Acts and Gender Constitution: An Essay in Phenomenology and Feminist Theory," *Performing Feminisms: Feminist Critical Theory and Theatre*, Ed. Sue-Ellen Case, Baltimore: Johns Hopkins UP, 1990.

3 Motherhood and Sexuality

In Chapter 1, 27 of the book of *Genesis of Old Testament*, woman was created together with man, and in the image of God. But it is again cited in Chapter 2, 22 of the same book that woman was created after man was created, and not from "the dust of the ground" like him, but from man's rib. In an attempt to explain this contradiction, Jewish tradition claims that the first woman was Lilith - a woman who was man's equal and devilish in her sexuality. Since she and man were fighting constantly, she left him and was copulating in deep waters with demons. She refused to return to man even when God threatened to have a hundred of her offspring die each day. Eve, man's second woman, was created from a rib because the rib is the most modest part of the body. Thus the split between motherhood and sexuality has revealed the deep ambivalence that characterises the two contradictory perceptions of a woman: A woman can either be motherly like Eve and then is pure, virgin, holy, and a support for her husband, or she can be sexual like Lilith, and then she is sinful, devilish, lacking any maternal instincts. This idea still has been held in our society that the more sexual a woman is perceived to be, the less she will be evaluated as a good mother.[1] According to Christopher L.C.E Witcombe, the legend of Lilith merges with the earlier legend of Sumero-Babylonian origin, dating from around 3,500 BCE.[2]

In patriarchal values there might be duality between sexuality and motherhood, and Lilith and Eve were two symbolic characters to represent patriarchal ideas on Motherhood.

In the first-wave and second-wave feminism, all feminists share a belief that women are enslaved by domesticity and defined by their roles as mother and wife. Betty Friedan called the family a 'comfortable concentration camp'.[3]

According to Simone De Beauvoir, the myths of women are created by the masculine world, and these myths (such as the myth of the mother, the virgin, the motherland, nature, etc.) attempt to trap woman into an impossible ideal by denying the individuality and situation of all different kinds of women.[4] Simone was against the motherhood and even against the marriage. It is no doubt that feminism was influenced by Marxism for a long time. Simone was influenced by the Hegelian 'others' theory and for a long time indirectly Hegel, Marx and Engels led the feminist movement.

Marx's early thinking was greatly influenced by that of Hegel and Feuerbach, characterised by idealism and humanism. The very concept of alienation came from idealist thought of early Marx, where he broke radically with every theory that based history and politics on an essence of man. The idea of commune concept developed by later Marxist activists was also based on this alienation concept where the idea of family structures and mother-hood responsibilities were denied. Marx believed that history was "determined" by changes in the relationship of production and consumption, and consumption was often a product of rhetorical pressures imposed by ideologies, which created a "false consciousness." But since then it is observed that one should not judge every human activities with production and consumption factor, and the relationship of mother and her offspring are the first example to refuse that production and consume theory.

In this prospect, I have to mention Simone again. She was somehow influenced by Marx (or to say pro-Marxian Hegelian theory). She categorically denied Motherhood. Betty Friedan wrote *The Feminine Mystique* in 1963, where she argued for abolishing the family, but in 1981, she again wrote *The Second Stage*, where she explained that her theories had been misunderstood. Friedan asked for a reconsideration of marriage. She pleaded for feminists to move away from anti-family rhetoric and back to a dialogue that addressed the needs of most women, who were wives and mothers. She called for a humanistic evolution that would enrich the institution of the family by including the needs and desires of men in the picture.

In the '70s Germaine Greer encouraged women for the revolutionary breakdown of sex roles. With her outrageous and shocking language, she proposed that women should refuse to marry. Being married, there might be every chance for a woman to become a subject for her role as a commodity in a capitalist society. But in a later book, however, she forthrightly defends a more traditional version of the family. She accepts the idea that a husband, wife and children constitute the basic familial unit.

The sexuality of a woman no doubt is repressed by motherhood because the sexual drive calls for active and immediate need gratification; motherhood requires sacrifice, passivity and postponement of gratification. But sex is not all for either in the life of man and woman. Motherhood brings some feminine sensuality which a woman can't rule out from her life. The desire for children is a feminine sensibility, and while considering all aspects, we should not overlook the emotional suffering of infertility, pregnancy loss, or still, birth sorrows of a female. It is true that motherhood makes a female limited to her sphere temporarily within the four walls of the home, and in the post-natal period, she has to take charge of child rearing. Who does not know that men are irresponsible and undependable when it comes to child care and housekeeping in India? A female has to bear financial loss at her workplace due to her pregnancy in an unorganised private sector. Personally I believe that all the theories made by the second and third-wave Western feminists on motherhood are denying women a basic choice about their womanhood and about their lives. I have marked, in the growing trend of feminism, the Western feminist thinkers like Simone, Friedan, Greer and even Linda Hirshman have a tendency to make feminism equal to the status of a patriarchal role. Patriarchal role in society is a devilish tradition implied by the masculine world and our attempts should not be to create another social milieu of exploitation and injustice. Feminism does not aim to destroy the family structure or to attack on the emotional bondage of love and passion. The motto of feminism should to create a new world with a new perspective of equality and humanist attitude. Feminism must be a road to glorify the female role with her own sensibilities. So, we can admit that being a mother is one of the most important jobs in the world, but we should also confirm that motherhood is not the only "choice" available to women. A woman should have the right to say "yes", as well as "no", to having children.

In South Asia, motherhood is always mingled with a religious and social goal of patriarchal society and is not subjected to a woman's wish but of man's. In Hinduism a 'son' is the 'must' requirement for a man to achieve his personal 'moksha' after his death. So the *Manu Smruti* stresses upon "putrarthe kriyate bharya", which means a wife is required to bear sons. This is the most insulting status of a woman in Hinduism, and an infertile woman loses her status in her family as well as in society. Such as woman is treated like a widow and is barred from any social rituals; many orthodox Hindus in rural areas still believe that encountering an infertile woman the first thing in the morning is a bad omen for the whole day. So, while discussing about motherhood in the South Asian perspective, we should not forget this status quo.

But I still believe that motherhood and sexuality are so closely connected to a woman's experience and woman's gender identity and that the idea of split between them is only a false myth woven by the patriarchal society.

Notes and References

1. Friedman, Ariella. Journal article, *Sex Roles: A Journal of Research*, Vol. 38, 1998.
2. The legend of Lilith as the "first Eve" merges with the earlier legend of Sumero-Babylonian origin, dating from around 3,500 BCE, of Lilith as a winged female demon who kills infants and endangers women in childbirth. In this role, she is one of several *mazakim* or "harmful spirits" known from incantation formulas preserved in Assyrian, Hebrew and Canaanite inscriptions intended to protect against them. As a female demon, she is closely related to Lamashtu whose evilness included killing children, drinking the blood of men, and eating their flesh. Lamashtu also caused pregnant women to miscarry, disturbed sleep and brought nightmares. 7th Chapter: Eve & Lilith: "Eve and the identity of women", Christopher L.C.E Witcombe, Sweet Briar College, Sweet Briar.

3 Friedan, Betty, *Feminine Mystique*, Norton, W. W. & Company, Inc, 1963.

4 Beauvoir, Simone de, *The Second Sex* (Written: in French and first published as Le Deuxième Sexe, in 1949), First Published in English: by Jonathan Cape, 1953.

4 Mother-Daughter Conflict

"To compound matters, I had a tempestuous relationship with my mother, and feared the inevitable kickback sure to follow such a final and dramatic departure from daughterhood. What if, instead of joy and excitement, my mother felt threatened by the baby, and pushed even further into the margins of my life? What if, then, out of jealousy and her own discontent, she launched covert or not-so-covert strikes against my irrefutable separateness, now symbolised so completely by becoming a mother myself?

Because mothers make us, because they map our emotional terrain before we even know we are capable of having an emotional terrain, they know just where to stick the dynamite. With a few small power plays—a sceptical comment, the withholding of approval or praise—a mother can devastate a daughter. Decades of subtle undermining can stunt a daughter, or so monopolise her energy that she in effect stunts herself. Muted, fearful, riddled with self-doubt, she can remain trapped in daughterhood forever, the one place she feels confident she knows the rules."

(Excerpt from Rebecca Walker's *Baby Love,* Riverhead Books, 2007).

The conflict between American mother-daughter feminists Alice Walker and Rebecca Walker is well known chapter for Western feminism. Alice Walker, the mother, the second wave feminist, obviously had an anti–motherhood ideas as the other Western feminists of her time. But Rebecca Walker, her daughter and a feminist of third wave discussed in her book *Baby Love* about how motherhood freed women like herself from their roles as daughters, and how this provided the much-needed perspective to heal themselves from damaged mother-daughter relationships and claim their full adulthood. What happened? This latest article is mired in unresolved childish hurt and anger (especially in the chapter "How my mother's fanatical views tore us apart"), which would be all well and good except that she strikes out at her mother by striking out at feminism. I personally think, the bitterness between her and her mother, as any woman who has ever fallen out with her mother knows, is a very painful experience and note to self, one that probably shouldn't be written about too much in public.

In her book *Baby Love*, Rebecca Walker writes directly about unadulterated excitement and pride about becoming a mother. She argues that motherhood frees us from childhood; it is the most important step a woman can take because it creates another human being and because it makes a woman an adult. I found this to be true for myself. In one of my stories, *Amruta Pratiksha Re* (Waiting for Manna)[1] (1989), published much more before the *Baby Love*, where I wanted to discuss the queries after a lifetime of wondering whether to have children, wondering if the sacrifices are worth it, wondering if life is full to bursting enough already and how our generation of women decides to have children.

I find myself nearer to Rebecca than to Alice on motherhood topic. I have told before that the motherhood-sexuality conflict is created by only Western feminists, but for me Alice' and Rebecca's conflict is a different issue from these motherhood-sexuality (or to say feminism) split. The conflict of mother and daughter sometimes creates the discomforts of their inequality by falling back on the motherhood mystique.

It is also a strange fact to note that Alice Walker always tried to avoid the conflict between her and Rebecca, in public. I think, the conflict between the two personalities is not due to theoretical inclination but rather due to a personal and psychological reason. Rebecca is a bisexual and was known for her relationship with Meshell Ndegeocello, but she became pregnant with her boyfriend and as a mother Alice perhaps couldn't bear this status. There are always hidden expectations on both sides. A mother has some expectations by which she tries to measure her daughter on that scale. She always wishes her daughter to be disciplined and expects her to do all those activities which she herself has not done in her life. Similarly, a daughter has also some expectations from her mother and she always thinks her mother too old to lead a personal life, and being youthful, getting attention from the public. These opposite polar thoughts make both mother and daughter possess ambivalent love/hate relationship.

There are competitions and jealousy which operate between every mother and her young adult daughter. They have tendencies to deny each other's private lives. I don't know practically what is the relation between mothers and daughters in the Western culture. I find it is quite natural for a family in the Western world, where a girl could invite her boyfriend to her home. But in the Eastern world, such possibilities are very rare happenings, and though the urban upper middle class people allow love marriages yet still dating of their daughter with her boyfriend always makes the parents keep it a secret from society, and a girl can't dare to invite her boyfriend to her drawing room. In such cases, it is a normal phenomenon that a girl can't imagine her mother to have had any extramarital relationship or her mother to have had any boyfriend. At the same time a mother also always dislikes finding her daughter spending long hours over the phone talking to any stranger. The fashionable dresses or make-up may also create jealousy in a mother's mind. But this is not all. I have witnessed a good friendship between mother and daughter, where the mother tries to fulfil her failed dreams through her daughter and we see a very unstylish mother trying to make her daughter more fashionable and smarter. In one of my stories *Agneya Giri* (*Volcano*) I tried to paint such a type of psychological agony of mother-daughter conflicts/ friendships.

The relation between a married daughter with her mother becomes even more critical, fragile and competitive. The married daughter is always considered by her mother as the 'other'. The mother and the daughter have two different families and their concerns are also different, hence more a sharing the utilities and jealousy develops at the same time. But this is wrong to say that the 'love' between mother and daughter is in a diminished stage after the marriage of the latter. In total scenario of Rebecca's blaming her mother depicts the jealousy, where Alice's mature mind as well as the 'love' for her daughter's career made her hide these tactfully from the public.

The mother of a young adult girl had to pass through two phases: girlhood and also as a daughter-in-law. At this phase she finds herself nearer to the gray-haired aged woman and is about to enjoy all freedoms that are meant for the masculine world. So when she mulls over her daughter's future life, she tries to mould her daughter so to cope in a daughter-in-law–hood environment without suffering any socio-psychological setback.

The social structures in the Eastern world demands the girl to act more as a daughter-in-law in a family than as a wife to someone. So unlike the Western girls the South Asian girls are commonly depicted as requiring veiling and modesty. There are dress decorum, speech censorship and even movement restrictions. For the married woman (in the case of a daughter-in-law), she has to cover her head while appearing before any stranger or elder person. A few decades ago, in the rural areas, they were not allowed to roam in the village lane. One can see that the rules were not so strict for unmarried girls and for the older women, who left their homes to roam village lanes with their heads and faces uncovered. Even the gray-haired aged women could roam publicly baring to the waist on hot days, without regard for showing their long-dry breasts. The younger adults' views of older women were that they had the power to limit a daughter-in-law's movements, to interfere with a son's marital intimacies, and the like; yet the older women usually speak of feeling that they were losing in the contest for a son's affection, loyalty and favour. Indian widowhood rarely distinguished between the consequences of widowhood for a woman in her youth and for a woman past menopause, although one can find striking differences. Older women were, in important ways, "like men," implying that what differentiates a "man" from a "woman" is not constant over the life course. This is, I think, a different social scenario, which makes South Asian feminism a distinct different from that of the Western one.

Western society has changed a lot since Jane Austen's *Pride and Prejudice*. Rather we can find a similar society that the novel depicted in Asian countries where the daughter's marriage still remains with the parent's responsibilities. In *The Joy Luck Club* (1989), by Amy Tan,[2] the characters Suyuan and June have a mother-daughter relationship fraught with conflict, but ultimately rooted in deep love and commitment for one another. Amy Tan, a Chinese American immigrant writer also focuses on the mother-daughter relationships in another novel, *The Kitchen God's Wife*. In my two short stories *Agnayagiri* (*Volcano*) and Dukha Apramita *(Sorrows Unending)*[3], I focus on the mother-daughter relationship. But in Western contemporary fictions the mother and daughter relationships appear on totally another dimension which is difficult to accept for an Eastern mind. For example, in the novel *The Horse Whisperer* by Nicholas Evans, the mother Annie falls in love with her daughter Grace's fiancé Tom. Relationships change due to mishaps, such as accidents leading to physical disabilities. In the novel, *The Horse Whisperer* by Nicholas Evans, the relationship between a mother and a daughter changes drastically for the better after the daughter is burdened with a physical disability and it creates a lot of mother-daughter conflict. This type of conflict though would not be ruled out in the Eastern social scenario, I think the mother-daughter conflict sources and responses among Western families are still not well understood. Conflict sources were mothers' unsolicited advice, daughters and mothers not living up to expectations of the other, and daughters' independence from mothers. Responses to conflict included voicing concerns, displaying loyalty and utilising the assistance of family. That is why the conflict between Alice Walker and Rebecca Walker is discussed, and suggestions for future research on mother-daughter conflict within the Western context are provided.

References

1. Sahoo, Sarojini. *Waiting for Manna.* (9788190695602). Vadodara: Indian AGE Communication, 2008.
2. Tan, Amy. *The Joy Luck Club.* G. P. Putnam's Sons, 1989
3. Sahoo, Sarojini. *Waiting for Manna.* (9788190695602). Vadodara: Indian AGE Communication, 2008.

5 The Marital Practice and Feminism

"When a subject is highly controversial—and any question about sex is that—one cannot hope to tell the truth. One can only show how one came to hold whatever opinion one does hold. One can only give one's audience the chance of drawing their own conclusions as they observe the limitations, the prejudices, the idiosyncrasies of the speaker."—Virginia Woolf.[1]

The word "chastity" refers to sexual purity and in Eastern ethics it is always linked with only woman and only with her self-denial of sexuality, tolerance, submissiveness and with an idea that here is no greater God than her husband. Never is any question asked or discussed any day on man's chastity, neither in the Western nor in the Eastern world. *The Quran*, allows polygamy for man but it does not allow that right for a woman and the Christian churches also deny polygamy for both man and woman; so too Hindu/Buddhist and other religions categorically deny the sexual rights of a woman. In every society, it is hoped that a woman should be chaste. Our society possesses a prejudice idea that women are more loose than men and so some 220 words exist in English for the sexually promiscuous woman, but only 22 for promiscuous men.[2]

Here I will discuss only our Eastern traditions, In India, with its strong bent for tradition, woman was expected mainly to live for others than for herself because "others" controlled and moulded the social structure. Woman in life and literature voluntarily surrendered to the ideal of self-sacrifice. Meena Shirwadkar writes "Sita (Rama's wife in the epic *Ramayana*) exemplifies the behaviour of the proper Hindu wife, devotedly following her husband into exile to the forest for twelve years, and eventually, after being kidnapped for a time by the evil Ravana whom Rama finally destroyed, proving her wifely virtue by placing herself on a lighted pyre. In some part of India, women annually worship Savitri, a goddess whose renown emanates from her extreme devotion to her husband, through which she saves him from the god of death. The story of Savitri is held up as a prime example of the lengths to which a wife should go in aiding her husband. The good wife saves her husband from death, follows him anywhere, proves her virtue, remains under his control and gives him her power."[3] In Hindu mythology Anasuya has been considered as Mahasati. According to *Garuda Purana*, being criticised by her leper husband Kaushika, she still considered him her deity and once instructed by her husband she took him to a prostitute, carrying also a lot of money and asked the prostitute to allow her husband to sleep with her.

Since the old Sangam period in South India, we find literature is used to glorify the chastity of woman ("karpu" in Tamil). In *Silappatikaram*, the famous Sangam epics (Professor A.L. Basham has translated this epic in English), Kannagi, the eternally suffering chaste wife, bore her husband`s unchasteful behaviour and killed herself after her husband's assassination by the king. She went to Heaven to reunite with her unchaste husband. This is the value that Indian patriarchal society possesses on sexual purity in marital life.

Once I read in the Asian Human Rights Commission's report that a woman in Rajasthan was found bleeding from her thighs, causing injuries due to her chastity belt.[4] The use of chastity belt is not common in India and it was also not originated in India. It appeared in Italy under Francesco II from Carrara, and was mostly used in Italy, but it suddenly spread all over France as well. Some argued that the instrument was aimed at preventing women from the possible risk of being raped, when their partner was away for a long time. It was also presented to a woman by her husband or lover in order to encourage her to be faithful. The patriarchal society always has double standards and the concept of such chastity belt may be the suitable example of their conspiracy. It became worse when widows were forced to be burnt with their late husbands on their funeral pyre in the name of "Sati System" in ancient India. Though this system is now prohibited by law, yet a few years ago when a twenty year old widow Roop Kanwar was dragged to the pyre of her demised husband, the question agitated the modern Indian mind that the roots of patriarchal hegemony is still deep-rooted anywhere in our cultural context.

Sexual purity is always clung with the purity of love. It is considered that sex is always mingled with love. In the Oriya version of the *Mahabharata* written by Sarala Das, it is stated that Draupadi had infatuations with Krishna and Karna; the latter was the illegitimate brother of the Pandavas. Draupadi had sexual relations with the five Pandavas, but still her heart was running after Krishna and Karna. This I think is the real picture of a woman's heart. For a woman the meaning of sex is very different from that of the man and I have discussed these matters later in this book in one of my essays, titled "Pleasure on Par".

The Hindu scholars might have forgotten that in Hindu mythology there are many examples of "free women" over "chaste women". There was no moral condemnation or belittling of "free women", and they also married and had children, but with a different social and familiar context. They were largely considered on par with men (not only with their men but with all men), not subject to father, husband and son, rather they were very respected in society. They were generally very learned, and normally sitting in public assemblies with men to discuss about the state's affairs. Many kshatriya ladies, even of royal families, were in this category. One of very known scripture in Sanskrit was that:

> Ahalya, Draupadi, Kunti, Tara Mandodari tatha
> Panca kanyd smarennityam mahdpataka nasanam

Ahalya, Draupadi, Kunti, Tara and Mandodari are five characters in mythology considered as the famous "Pancha Kanyas" (five Virgins) and interestingly enough none of them were monogamous (I have discussed about their relationship in my earlier article *Pleasure at Par*. So the status of these five free ladies was no lesser than that of Sati, Savitri or Anasuya. Actually Hinduism is not a religion in which sense Greco-Semitic religions are. It is a cluster of ideas, philosophy and lifestyles. Here, every contradictory idea may remain side by side claiming its authenticity. The most atheist Charvak is also considered as a great sage in Hindu cult. So, it is foolish to blame Hinduism for any particular idea. I think Hinduism allows all to lead their life according to their own beliefs, and it respects and regards all types of lifestyle. Hence, it is the time when we can think over the "free woman" status in our Eastern society to check the patriarchal dominancy over the female world.

Opposite to monogamy the heterosexual relationships are multi-termed activities such as polygamy, polyandry, polygyny and polyamory. "Polygamy" is a marital practice in which a person has more than one spouse simultaneously; "polyandry" refers to a form of polygamous marriage, or other sexual union, in which one woman is married to two or more husbands at the same time. "Polygyny", on the other hand, refers to polygamy in which one man has two or more wives.

Monogamy is always a double standard activity by males. It is deliberately an extremist idea which is built into its core rule that men can have multiple spouses but women cannot. Even worse, traditional polygamy is always used as a form of polygyny and female sexuality gets exploited. Women these days expect and demand to have the same standing in relationships as men. Polygamy denies this and women find a lesser status in such traditional polygamy. In case polygamy turns to polyandry, then also we find woman is sexually used by men or very soon she is rejected by her lover. The purity of love and the emotional bondage does not act in monogamy. On the other hand, by allowing monogamy we make ourselves confined to a double standard system created by the masculine world. The traditional monogamy once made the 'widows' to lead a tortuous life, wearing of a white sari, adopting vegan food habits and leaving all sorts of feminine aestheticism in the name of "satvik" life whereas there were no such rules for any widower any day.

The poet Ezra Pound once observed (somewhat self-servingly) that artists are the "antennae of the race." These antennae have long been jolting about extramarital affairs. It seems that every great literary tradition, either in the Eastern or in the Western world, finds it especially fascinating to explore monogamy's failures. The old Western epics like, Homer's *Iliad*, recounts the failure of monogamy: Helen's face launched a thousand ships and changed the course of history only after it first launched an affair between Helen, a married woman and Greek queen, and Paris, son of King Priam of Troy. Helen proceeded to leave her husband Menelaius, thereby precipitating the Trojan War. And in the *Odyssey*, we learn of Ulysess's return from that war, whereupon he slays a virtual army of suitors, each of whom was trying to seduce his faithful wife, Penelope. Some of the examples of modern classics from Western literature are: Tolstoy's *Anna Karenina*, Flaubert's *Madame Bovary*, Lawrence's *Lady Chatterly's Lover*, Hawthorne's *The Scarlet Letter*, Henry James's *The Golden Bowl*. And even in a later period, we find John Updike and others.

Now one can ask a question: is it possible to be in love with more than one person at a time? The traditional answer may be "No", but if we think over the issue more seriously we can have an affirmative answer. Virtually a human heart is a multi-chambered space where every chamber is allotted to a person. We have kept a reserved space for our spouse, parents, children, relatives, friends, neighbours and even for our colleagues, and if we can equally love them, it is doubtless that a person can allot more seats for 'lovers'. In 1983, Blumstein and Schwartz tried to survey 3,574 Western married couples in their sample and found 15-28 per cent had "an understanding that allows non-monogamy under some circumstances. The percentages were higher among cohabitating couples and they even found the percentages were higher among cohabitating couples (28%), lesbian couples (29%) and gay male couples (65%)."[5]

In 1999, Morning Glory Zell-Ravenheart was asked by the editor of the *Oxford English Dictionary* to provide a definition of the term (which the dictionary had not previously recognised). The words "polyamory/ous/ist" were formally added to the *OED* in 2006. The Ravenhearts defined and expanded the term as follows:

> The practice, state or ability of having more than one sexual loving relationship at the same time, with the full knowledge and consent of all partners involved.

This term was meant to be inclusive, and in that context, we have never intended to particularly exclude "swinging" *per se*, if practitioners thereof wished to adopt the term and include themselves. The two essential ingredients of the concept of polyamory are more than one; and loving. That is, it is expected that the people in such relationships have a loving emotional bond, are involved in each other's lives multidimensionally, and care for each other. This term is not intended to apply to merely casual recreational sex, anonymous orgies, one-night stands, pick-ups, prostitution, "cheating," serial monogamy, or the popular definition of swinging as "mate-swapping" parties.

Swinging, sometimes referred to as the swinging lifestyle, is non-monogamous sexual activity, treated much like any other social activity, that can be experienced as a couple.... Whore redirects here...."[6]

Polyamory is a word which is often confused with polygamy and polyandry. In the *Mahabharata*, the Pandavas are married to one common wife, Draupadi. What would I say to it? Polyandry or Polyamory? It is a strange fact that nobody asked Draupadi about her wish before her such marriage. Except Robert Heinlein's science fiction *The Moon Is a Harsh Mistress*, I haven't found any instance of any polyamory relationships neither in our myths or epics nor in modern literature in both Western or Eastern society. The movies 'Three of Hearts: A Postmodern Family' is a 97-minute long Susan Kaplan's film, starring Steven Margolin, Sam Cagnina (II), and Samantha Singh. It was shown in Miami International Film Festival in March of 2005 under the Documentary Film Section is considered to be only one of its kind on polyamory.

Neither in the East nor West, in the society ever allowed this type of relationship as still the patriarchal claims over woman as a property exists in some hidden form. The orthodox Christian and Islam beliefs still prevailed in the society of both Eastern and Western worlds. *Quran* allows polyandry but it does not allow polyamory, and so too the Christian churches deny both polyandry and polyamory. In every society, it is hoped that a woman should keep her chastity pure. In modern Indian society, though this practice prevails, except for the eminent poetess Amrita Pritam, nobody would dare to accept this relationship publicly.

Not much is also known by the psychology field concerning polyamory. Our textbooks on family functioning don't mention it, our diverse literature don't incorporate it, and many members of the polyamory community have reported encounters with therapists who are uninformed at best, or biased at worst, about this lifestyle. Geri D. Weitzman, a social psychologist who claims herself as a polyamorous woman, presented a paper at the 8th Annual Diversity Conference on March 12th, 1999 in Albany, New York, where she tried to prove that the negative view of polyamorous individuals that some therapists have expressed is borne out by empirical data and added that polyamory is a valid and healthy lifestyle; however, just as there are stressers associated with being gay or bisexual in a heterosexual society, so are there stressers associated with being polyamorous in a monogamous society.[7]

References

1. Woolf, Virginia, *A Room of One's Own*, England: Hogarth Press, 1929.
2. Bernard, Jessie, *The Female World 1*. New York: Free Press, 1981, pp. 376-384.
3. Shirwadkar, Meena, "Women and the Hindu Tradition," *Women in India*, (New Delhi: Manohar, 1986, pp.122-123.
4. "A Statement by the Asian Human Rights Commission." (AHRC) and published in WLUML (*Women Living Under Muslim Laws*) *Newsletter-4* (August 2007).
5. Rubin, A. M., & Adams, J. R., "Outcomes of sexually open marriages", *The Journal of Sex Research*, 22(3), 311-319. (1986).
6. Flood, Michael, *The Men's Bibliography: A comprehensive bibliography of writing on men, masculinities, gender, and sexualities*, Canberra, Australia. 19th edition, 2008.
7. Ravenscroft, Anthony, *Polyamory: roadmaps for the clueless and hopeful: an introduction on polyamory*. Santa Fe, NM: Fenris Brothers, 2004.

6 The Vagina Monologues

The Vagina Monologues is the famous episodic play of America, written by Eve Ensler, which ran at the off-Broadway Westside Theatre and at HERE Arts Center in 1996. Later a television version featuring Ensler was produced by cable TV channel HBO. It has been performed in 76 countries. In 2003 it was first performed in India (Mumbai) and was produced by Poor-box productions. In 2004, it was banned in Chennai. The play was translated into Hindi and was first performed in January 2007 under the title of "Yoni ki baat". Ensler made up different monologues read by a different women. Initially, Eve Ensler performed every monologue herself, with subsequent performances featuring three actresses, and more recent versions featuring a different actress for every role. Later she turned it to perform annually and a new monologue is added to highlight a current issue affecting women around the world. Every monologue somehow relates to the women, be it through sex, love, rape, menstruation, mutilation, masturbation, birth, orgasm, the variety of names for the physical aspect of woman's body. A recurring theme throughout the piece is the vagina as a tool of female empowerment, and the ultimate embodiment of individuality. In 1998, Ensler announced to change Valentine Day to 'V-Day which stands for Vagina, Violence, and Victory', linking love and respect for women to ending violence against women and girls.

The Vagina Monologues, as having a negative and restrictive view of sexuality and an anti-male bias, impose a stress on hatred of men and heterosexuality. I have noted that, in the Western world, many feminist thinkers oppose male-female sexual relationships. They describe it as negative and destructive to women, whereas all female-female sexual relationships, even the one including statutory rape, are depicted as positive and nurturing. In *The Little Coochie Snorcher that Could*, an episode from *Vagina Monologue*, a thirteen-year-old girl recounts being given alcohol and then having sex with an adult woman; the incident is recalled fondly by the grown girl, who closes the monologue with the line, "If it was rape, it was good rape." Later, the "good rape" line was removed from the script, the girl's age was changed to sixteen, and warnings were issued to individuals putting on the play using older scripts containing the line which constituted a copyright violation and ground for legal action.

For many feminist thinkers, after marriage a family breeds patriarchy. Happily married women are considered false and double-crossing. The titles of popular feminist books from the early movement highlight the split between gender feminists and women who chose domesticity. Jill Johnston in her *Lesbian Nation* (1973),[1] called the married women heterosexual females who were 'traitors'; Kate Millett in her *Sexual Politics* (1970)[2] redefined heterosexual sex as a power struggle; whereas in Kathrin Perutz's *Marriage is Hell* (1972)[3] and Ellen Peck's *The Baby Trap* (1971),[4] they argued motherhood blocks liberation of a woman. These feminists always try to paint the marriage as legalised prostitution; heterosexual intercourse as rape; and they come to the decision that men are the enemy; families are prisons.

In my last article, I have shown how these feminists (Betty Friedan, Germaine Greer) have tried to skip from their anti marriage ideas in a later period. Marriage is a three-sided arrangement between a husband, a wife and society. That is, society legally defines what a marriage is and how it can be dissolved. But marriage is, on the other hand, for partners of marriage. It is more of an individual relationship than a social matter. This is the main reason of the crisis. Individually, I think, marriage must be taken out of the social realm and taken fully back into the private one. Society should withdraw from marriage and allow the adults involved to work out their own definition of justice in the privacy of their own homes.

Our feminist thinkers always try to skip the idea that offspring begging is a natural instinct of a woman, and it is related to our ecological and environmental situation. Anything against it may result in disaster. We find that a woman has to pass through a different stages in her lifespan and there is a phase where a woman feels an intense need of her own offspring. Feminists of the second-wave feminism have always tried to pursue a woman against the natural law because it seemed to them that motherhood is a barricade against the freedom of a woman. But if the woman has her own working field, d sn't it mean that her working assignments would demand more of her time, of her sincerity and, of course, her freedom? If a woman can adjust herself and can sacrifice her freedom for her own identity outside her home, then why shouldn't she sacrifice some of her freedom for parenting, when parenting is also a part of one of her social identity?And it could also be solved by rejecting the patriarchal role of parenting. We have to insist on the idea of division of labour in parenting. This equally shared parenting is now common in the West, but still in South Asian countries we find it a taboo factor because of economic inequality between men and women, our crazy work culture, and the constrictions that are placed on us by traditional gender roles.

Still in India, in a majority of the cases it stands in sharp contrast to the traditional marriage with children, in which the man works and the woman stays home, or the 'supermom' marriage, in which the man works and the woman tries to balance a career with the lion's share of the childcare and household tasks. Equally shared parenting is more than an extension of feminism; it is more than simply what is fair. Equally sharing the care of your children with your partner is about balancing your life, balancing your family's collective life and sharing equally in the joys of raising a family.

We again came to that point where we have to agree with the theory which states that economic inequality between men and women are the main barricade to solve the gender inequalities and not the marital practice or motherhood, as the Western feminist always tries to paint. Our motto should be to change our marriage system from the political realm to the private one. The new slogan of feminism should be 'the personal is personal.'

References

1. Johnston, Jill, *Lesbian Nation*, Simon and Schuster New York, NY, 1973.
2. Millett, Kate, *Sexual Politics*, Doubleday, New York, 1970.
3. Perutz, Kathrin, *Marriage is Hell*, Morrow, NY, 1972.
4. Peck, Ellen, *The Baby Trap*, David McKay Co, 1971.

7 Is Sexuality Mystic?

Ariel Levy, in her book Female *Chauvinist Pigs: Women and the Rise of Raunch Culture*[1], states that there are two types of feminists: "lipstick feminists" and "loophole women." According to Levy, lipstick feminists believe, for example, that stripping is empowering, and that putting on a show to attract men (be it through makeup, clothing, or girl-on-girl gyration) is not contrary to the goals and ideals of feminism. Levy disagrees with this view. It is interesting to find that the *Playboy* magazine and the *Femina* (the magazine which sponsored and organised beauty contest for India) are run by women. Levy named these as "raunch culture" in which women internalise objectifying male views of themselves and other women.

Feminists like Catharine MacKinnon (1987), Germaine Greer (1999), Pamela Paul (2005), and Dorchen Leidholdt (1990) argue that sex positive ideas[2] have historically benefited men rather than women and that, thus, the indiscriminate promotion of all kinds of sexual practices merely contributes to female oppression. Even in Eve Ensler's *The Vagina Monologues*, a negative view of sexuality is shown emphasizing sexual violence against women rather than the redemptive value of female sexuality.

As far back as 1935 Margaret Mead wrote about the need for freer sex roles. Mead, as an anthropologist, believed that women should be able to take part in more activities usually associated with men. From the 1960s, the idea of free sex immersed with third wave feminists and there was a 'Feminist Sex War'[3] among anti-pornography feminists and sex positive feminist started from the 1980s, when Andrea Dworkin and Robin Morgan attempted to place pornography at the centre of the feminist explanation for women's oppression. Sex positive feminists oppose any legal or social efforts to control sexual adventures and activities between consenting adults, and they stand firmly behind sexual minority groups like homosexuals, bisexuals, transgender, and cross dressers. As the most of the sex positive feminists are either bisexual (like Camille Paglia and Susie Bright) or lesbians, they focus more on these alternate sexual behaviour than heterosexual activities and men don't necessarily embody a problem and aren't typified as the oppressor. Another result of this social movement was that sex-positive feminists merely catered to men's desires because of the sexist notion that only men can enjoy sex in the first place. The third point which made sex positive feminism a controversial subject is that it admits and encourages pornography, BDSM[4] and prostitution, as (according to them) they are healthy, and fun. But accepting sex as fun and healthy does not require accepting violence, humiliation though they have been sexualised over the years by these activities in the centuries- long patriarchal tradition. and the culture at large.

In this so-called 'sex war', I think, the actual importance of the issues like 'sexual freedom of a woman 'or 'woman's right over her body' had been demoralised and become insignificant.. The sex-negative feminists often forget that they accept the sex-negative characterisation of feminism that has been imposed on us by people who are not feminists, and who in fact are generally our opponents. On the other hand, the sex-positive feminists also always forget that the value of sex depends on the people involved, what they want to get out of it, whether they're able to achieve that, and whether they are causing harm to themselves or others. That requires the ability to think again while they are supporting pornography or prostitutions or BDSM.

Sex never was introduced first in human history as a tool for any exploitation or any hegemony. Sexuality is always an integral part of the personality of every human being. Its full development depends upon the sharing of the satisfaction of basic human needs such as the desire for contact, intimacy, emotional expression, pleasure, tenderness and love.

Never does any idea of feminism support the portrayal of women as sexualised objects catering solely to man's needs. But it is also a fact that feminism's primary concerns is a woman's life and respect for her body. By denying the role of sex, we are indirectly denying the women the rights over their body. My argument for sex is not in favour of pornography or with BDSM. I consider sex as the possibility of women and men engaging as 'equals' whereas pornography usually dishonours women, men, children or even animals. I have stated before that feminism should not be considered as being gynocentric and misandrist any day, and it should be aimed at full civil and legal equality for women.

The state, society and judiciary can never accept sex for any purpose other than reproduction. But in art and literature sex always played a vital role and it keeps itself away from pornography. Could we call all the classic erotica from *Kumara Sambhava* of Kalidas to *Ulysses* of Joyce as porno? Could we put these writings as objectifying female as only a sexual tool? The erotica described in these literature involves emotions, love, passion and tender sensations; while a pornography involves lust, carnal desires and sexual excitement with no emotional ties.

In 6th century BC, Mutta, a female disciple of Buddha, wrote: "So free am I, so gloriously free, free from three petty things—from mortar, from pestle and from my twisted lord."[5] Translated from Pali, this text proves the first attempts of an Indian women to choose religious escapism as the only way out for those who were frustrated with a life inside the home. Mutta asked these women to join the Buddhist sangha (religious communities) in their attempts to break away from the social world of tradition and marriage. I think, perhaps this is the first poem about freedom of a woman from household chores and sexual slavery.

Although the early forms of writing addressed the issue of personal freedom, the poetry that followed later was a celebration of womanhood and sexuality. The Sangam poets that dominated the era between ca. 100 BC and AD 250 wrote extensively about what it meant to have a female body. The translation of Venmanipputi Kuruntokai's *What she said to her girlfriend* reads:

> On the banks shaded by a punnai clustered with flowers, when we made love my eyes saw him and my ears heard him; my arms grow beautiful in the coupling and grow lean as they come away.[6]

The content of the poem is bold for its time because it is expressing a woman's pleasure in sex. The poems written around this age echo a sense of sexual liberation.

In 12th century AD, the social and spiritual revolution of Akka Mahadevi, the Kannada Bhakti woman saint, can be considered as an attempt to liberate woman from sexual male hegemony. She was married to a local king Kaushika, but found herself in love with Lord Shiva, and ran away from her life of luxury to live as a wandering poet-saint, travelling throughout the region and singing praises to her beloved Shiva. She refused to wear any clothing by saying: "When all the world is the eye of the Lord, on looking everywhere, what can you cover and conceal?"[7]

At the World Congress of Sexology, held in Hongkong on August 26, 1999, the following rights were recommended to add as a part of Fundamental Human Rights:

1. *The right to sexual freedom.* Sexual freedom encompasses the possibility for individuals to express their full sexual potential. However, this excludes all forms of sexual coercion, exploitation and abuse at any time and situations in life.
2. *The right to sexual autonomy, sexual integrity and safety of the sexual body.* This right involves the ability to make autonomous decisions about one's sexual life within a context of one's own personal and social ethics. It also encompasses control and enjoyment of our own bodies free from torture, mutilation and violence of any sort.
3. *The right to sexual privacy.* This involves the right for individual decisions and behaviors about intimacy as long as they do not intrude on the sexual rights of others.
4. *The right to sexual equity.* This refers to freedom from all forms of discrimination regardless of sex, gender, sexual orientation, age, race, social class, religion, or physical and emotional disability.
5. *The right to sexual pleasure.* Sexual pleasure, including autoeroticism, is a source of physical, psychological, intellectual and spiritual well being.
6. *The right to emotional sexual expression.* Sexual expression is more than erotic pleasure or sexual acts. Individuals have a right to express their sexuality through communication, touch, emotional expression and love.
7. *The right to sexually associate freely.* This means the possibility to marry or not, to divorce, and to establish other types of responsible sexual associations.
8. *The right to make free and responsible reproductive choices.* This encompasses the right to decide whether or not to have children, the number and spacing of children, and the right to full access to the means of fertility regulation.
9. *The right to sexual information based upon scientific i quiry.* This right implies that sexual information should be

generated through the process of unencumbered and yet scientifically ethical inquiry, and disseminated in appropriate ways at all societal levels.

10. *The right to comprehensive sexuality education.* This is a lifelong process from birth throughout the life cycle and should involve all social institutions.
11. *The right to sexual health care.* Sexual health care should be available for prevention and treatment of all sexual concerns, problems and disorders.

Since historically, marriage has mostly been another way to barter and trade 'goods' and since many women in our societies still live under this oppressive model, admission of these sexual rights only can rescue them from the worse situation. On the other hand, the so-called 'raunch culture' makes woman nothing more than a product. If we once adopt 'sexuality' away from this so-called 'raunch culture' concept, we find the individual achievement in one's life, what Mutta or Akka Mahadevi have had in history. Sexuality is the pure form of human realisation and it is the factor responsible to enhance our creativity. That is why despite the blockage attempts of society, state and judiciaries, sexuality has its own role in art and that is why we find poets, writers, artists, musicians and others in creative professions more likely to exhibit a tendency toward sexual affinity in their lives. Nietzsche also shared this thought in his *Will to Power*, where he says, "The force that one expends in the artistic creation is the same as that expended in the sexual act: there is only one kind of force." This is why he thinks the (male) artist is typically quite chaste.

Notes and References

1. Levy, Ariel, *Female Chauvinist Pigs: Women and the Rise of Raunch Culture,* Free Press, August 30, 2005.
2. Glick, Elisa, "Sex Positive: Feminism, Queer theory and the Politics of Transgression, *Feminist Review-64,* Spring 2000.

3. Some of the feminists became involved in the sex-positive feminist movement in response to efforts by anti-pornography feminists like Catharine MacKinnon (1987), Germaine Greer (1999), Pamela Paul (2005), and Dorchen Leidholdt (1990) to put pornography at the centre of a feminist explanation of women's oppression. This period of intense debate and acrimony between sex-positive and anti-pornography feminists during the early 1980s is often referred to as the "Feminist Sex Wars". See: Duggan, Lisa, Hunter, Nan D. (1995), *Sex wars: sexual dissent and political culture.* New York: Routledge.
4. BDSM is a complex acronym derived from the terms bondage and discipline, dominance and submission, sadism and masochism. Tying up (bondage), whipping, other kinds of beatings, and various other forms of pain, certain kinds of humiliation are quite common in this kind of sex. It is essentially a form of playful 'power exchange'. See Miller, Phillip; Devon, Molly and Granzig, William A., *Screw the Roses, Send Me the Thorns: The Romance and Sexual Sorcery of Sadomasochism*, Mystic Rose Books 1995, p. 95.
5. Tharu, Susie and Lalita, K. (Eds), *Women Writing in India*, Volume 1, 600 BC to the Early Twentieth Century, Oxford University Press, New Delhi. 1991, p.68
6. Ibid., p.73.
7. Nandakumar, Prema, "Vachanas of Madadevi Akka", the review of the book *Mahadevi Akkavin Arulmozhigal* (Mahadevi Akka's Words of Grace), Book Review page of *The Hindu*, Tuesday, Nov. 16, 2004 issue.
8. See "Sexual Science": The Newsletter of the Society for the *Scientific Study of Sexuality*, Spring 1999, Volume 40 - Issue 2.

8 Mythical Sexual Politics

As the term 'myth' may suggest, it is something which is absurd or fictional. Or is it?

While these beliefs and stories need not be a literal account of actual events, they may yet express ideas that are perceived by some people and cultures to be truths at a deeper or more symbolic level. The word 'myth' comes from the Greek word "mythos." The Greek Lexicon, *Liddell and Scott*, defines "mythos" as: word and speech.[1]

In his essay "Did the Greeks Believe Their Myths?" Paul Veyne writes: "Myth is truthful, but figuratively so. It is not historical truth mixed with lies; it is a high philosophical teaching that is entirely true, on the condition that, instead of taking it literally, one sees in it an allegory."[2]

In *The Golden Bough* (1890), Sir James George Frazer writes that all myths were originally connected with the idea of fertility in nature, with the birth, death, and resurrection of vegetation as a constantly recurring motif.[3]

It is very interesting to note when we cook into the Mesopotamian, Greek and Hindu civilisations, that even though religions and cultures existed in different parts of the world and were separated by great distances and time, yet there are some amazing similarities between their fables and myths. The concept of goddess always lies with sexuality and we find great similarities in all the myths of goddesses worldwide. In Sumer, the goddess was known as Inanna, and in Babylon and

Assyria, she was known as Ishtar. She was Aphrodite for the Greeks. The Egyptians called her Hathor, Quaddesha and Aset. To the Phoenicians, she was Astarte. To the Hebrews, she was Ashtoreth and Ashera. And to the Philistines, she was Atergatis.

Though in all these cultures, sex is so suppressed in social conversation that if any one tries to have a conversation about sex or sexuality, some may think of it as "dirty" or "perverted." But in case of myths (if we consider myths as tales of the people), we find that a fascination towards sexual orientation has made these myths more attached to sexual fantasies than to other aspects of life. In his book *Gay Witchcraft: Empowering the Tribe,* Christopher Penczak, an author in the fields of paganism and magic, has elaborately discussed some gods and goddesses created by these myths with the sexual fantasies. For instance, the Greek king Oedipus unwittingly married his mother after killing his father, pulling out his eyes when he discovered their identity. The Candomble deity Orungan ravished his mother, Yemanja, who then gave birth to a dozen children as well as the sun and the moon. In one version of the Aztec myth about their mother goddess, Coatlique's husband physically abused her until one of her several hundred sons took action, killing his father and becoming his mother's lover. The South American Panare mythology contains an example of father-daughter incest: Whenever the Sun and his daughter, the Moon, have intercourse, there is a total eclipse. Zeus, who occasionally dallied with handsome human males, was so sexually voracious that he would be positioned near the boiling centre of the circle or in other words, at the torrid "heat" of sexual passion. Poseidon, the Greek god of the seas, was not far behind Zeus in his sexual proclivities. He ravished numerous women including the goddess Demeter. He raped Amphitrite, although he later married her.

In mythology, the gods are often transsexual or can switch sexes in an instant. For example, there is the Balinese god, Syng

Hyang Toenggal; a Hindu equivalent would be Indra, the transgendered sky god; and the Nordic equivalent would be the two-gendered Ymir, whose sacrifice was necessary for the creation of the Earth. Quan Yin, the Chinese goddess of compassion, is often pictured with Buddha. She is seen as beyond human conceptions of male or female, and can change her gender at will, as the occasion demands. Hermaphroditus, the son of Aphrodite and Hermes, is a hermaphrodite, giving his name to those whose physiology incorporates both a penis and female breasts. The concept of Ardhanarishwara, the "ambisexual" creator god in Hindu mythology, is also compared with the Aztec god Ometecuhtli, who could give birth to the deities of the four directions. Candomble, an African-Brazilian religion, venerates Oxala, the "ambisexual" god of purity and wisdom. Baron Samedi, the Vodoun deity both of death and sexuality, typically is portrayed wearing both male and female garments, and is often pictured inviting men to engage in anal intercourse with him. Another "ambisexual" Vodoun deity is Damballah, the god of rainbows, peace, and prosperity.[4]

In the northern area of Sumeria known as Akkadia, later called Babylonia, women were not confined to the home but instead had a role to play in public life. This was especially true of the priestesses, who owned property and transacted business. Property from family estates was inherited equally by sisters and brothers. A daughter, when she married, was given a dowry that she was allowed to keep in the event of a divorce. Sometime around 2300 BC, all this began to change. The patriarchal form of society began to empower more, and the masculine world took a more authoritarian role. A woman might still own property but it was no longer hers to dispose of freely. Now she must first consult her husband and obtain his permission. When Hammurabi formulated his code known as the Code of Hammurabi in around 1760 BC, the position of women had obviously been greatly eroded. Sarah Dening[5], the noted dream expert of noted Kingdom, tries to shape sexual roles in different social sequences cited above through myths in her much acclaimed book *The Mythology of Sex*.[6]

Dening pointed her finger to the Sumerian myth of Inanna. She was the goddess of love and procreation, similar to the Hindu goddess Rati Devi, Anath of Canaan, Isis of Egypt, and the Babylonian goddess, Ishtar. All these goddesses were rejoiced in their sexuality. Inanna is often depicted resting her foot on the back of a lion, offering the king the symbolic objects indicating his ruling power. Lions, when associated with feminine deities, represent the other side of their character manifesting undomesticated, fierce, aggressive aspect of the female like the Hindu deity Durga.

Although Inanna was the goddess of love and sexuality, she was also called the Mother of Harlots and the Great Whore of Babylon, and she declared of herself as a prostitute. Her holy city of Erech was known as "the town of the sacred courtesans." In no way, therefore, was prostitution in the Babylonian era considered a shameful profession. On the contrary, temples to Ishtar were inhabited by sacred prostitutes or priestesses known as Ishtartu or Joy-Maidens, dedicated to the service of the goddess. Their sexuality was seen as belonging to her, to be used therefore only in the sacred rites undertaken in her worship. Indeed, the original meaning of the word "prostitute" was "to stand on behalf of," that is, to represent, the power of the goddess.[7] Curiously perhaps, from a contemporary standpoint, Ishtar was often referred to as "Virgin," implying that her creativity and power were self-engendered and not dependent upon masculine power.

Unlike the Devdasi system among ancient Hindus where the unmarried maid disciples got married to the gods, in Babylonian culture, the priestesses would undertake the sacred marriage with any male worshipper who wanted union with the goddess. The man, whom the priestess had not met before and would not meet again, spent the night with her in the temple precincts. Their intercourse would put him in contact with the rejuvenating energy of the Goddess, mediated through her priestess who would bestow on him an ecstatic experience. For the priestess, the sexual act represented a ritual offering to the goddess. A very real benefit was therefore enjoyed by all concerned, not least the temple itself which could expect to earn considerable income from such worshippers. Apart from their sexual and commercial activities, temple prostitutes demonstrated considerable gifts in other areas. Because their natural secretions were considered to have a beneficial effect, they were greatly respected as healers of the sick. One clay tablet dating from this era tells us that diseases of the eye can be cured by a harlot's spittle. These women also acted as seers and were skilled in sorcery and prophecy.[8]

As a result, priestesses often engaged in commerce and might be involved in import and export, land management, and other profitable endeavors. The modern brothel of our own culture, with its "madam," might perhaps be seen as a somewhat pale reflection of the temple of Ishtar.

According to author Sarah Dening, the myths of Inanna were created when patriarchal milieus had not been in dominant form.

After Hammurabi, comes another myth, the Sumero-Babylonian Epic of Gilgamesh. Enkidu and Gilgamesh were two friends having a homosexual relationship. Later they meet the goddess Ishtar, who offers to marry Gilgamesh, promising him untold delights. He, however, preferring his friend Enkidu, rejects her advances in a deeply insulting way, referring to her in derogatory terms:

> Listen to me while I tell the tale of your lovers. There was Tammuz, the lover of your youth. For him you decreed wailing, year after year. You loved the many-coloured roller, but still you struck and broke his wing. You have loved the lion tremendous in strength: seven pits you dug for him, and seven.

> You have loved the stallion magnificent in battle, and for him, you decreed the whip and spur and a thong. You have loved the shepherd of the flock; he made meal-cake for you day after day and he killed kids for your sake. You struck and turned him into a wolf; now his own herd-boys chase him away. His own hounds worry his flanks.[9]

Enraged, Ishtar asks her father to create a heavenly bull to destroy the insolent hero. Gilgamesh and Enkidu kill the bull and Enkidu throws its organs into Ishtar's face. This is too much for the assembly of the gods, who decide that Enkidu must die. This will be the punishment that Gilgamesh must bear. Later, Enkidu is allowed to emerge from the underworld for a visit and Gilgamesh begs him to reveal what death is like.

Aphrodite was the Greek goddess of love and beauty, and was famous for her erotic nature. When we compare Ishtar with Aphrodite, we find the former is more free to have her will than the latter. For example, Ishtar was never forced to sleep with anyone against her will, but in the case of Aphrodite, we find she had to sleep with many gods even against her will. Ironically, Aphrodite was wedded to Hephaestus, who was lame and considered to be the most unattractive of all the gods. This marriage was through no choice of her own, but instead, was arranged by Zeus in order to keep Aphrodite out of trouble. The goddess of love did not take her wedding vows very seriously and was accustomed to having many affairs involving both gods and men. She had constant relations with Mars. Her children by Mars were Harmonia, Deimos (Fear) and Phobos (Panic). She was also the mother of Hermaphroditus with Mercury (Hermes), Priapus with Dionysus (Bacchus), and Beroe (after whom the city Berytus in Lebanon was named) with Adonis. Aphrodite was also the mother of Eryx and Rhodes by Poseidon, Aeneas and Lyrus with Anchises (a mortal king killed by Zeus for drunkenly telling of his affair with Venus), Astynois with Phaethon (a beautiful young boy whom Venus ravished), Eryx with Butes (of Jason and the Argonauts), and Eros (Cupid) and Anteros (the avenging spirit of spurned love) by unknown fathers.

Referring to the transformation of ethical values of myths with the change of milieus in society, Dening writes, "Given that myths tend to reflect aspects of the culture prevalent at the time, we may surmise that intimate relationships between men were not considered unusual. This could perhaps be expected in a society where archaeological evidence has shown that women had, by now, a very inferior role. Dual standards existed for married life, where a wife might be put to death for adultery, while a husband was free to enjoy as many women as he chose, provided he did not seduce the wife of another man."[10]

If the myths are in any way to be considered as the reflection of 'social ideas' of any group or society, then we can say that with the development of patriarchal control over feminine civil rights, the sexual freedom described in those myths was cut down from the women's world and transferred to the men's world with anti-feminist moral milieus which gradually made the female a sex object, however powerful they might be in their goddess perspectives. This is a valid point, I believe, that the sex negative feminists have to think of before raising their voice against the sex role attitudes of the female.

Notes and References

1. *Liddell and Scott Greek-English Lexicon* is the world's most authoritative dictionary of ancient Greek. Indispensable for biblical and classical studies alike, the world's most comprehensive and authentic word list. An Intermediate Greek-English Lexicon, (7th edition). Oxford University Press, USA; December 31, 1945.
2. Veyne, Paul (1988). *Did the Greeks Believe in Their Myths? An Essay on Constitutive Imagination.* (translated by Paula Wissing). University of Chicago.
3. *The Golden Bough: A Study in Magic and Religion* is a wide-ranging, comparative study of mythology and religion, written by Scottish anthropologist Sir James George Frazer. The book was originally

published in two volumes in 1890.Now it is available with Touchstone, published in December 1, 1995, ISBN-13: 978-0684826301.

4. Penczak, Christopher, *Gay witchcraft: Empowering the tribe,* Red Wheel/ Weiser, Boston, 2003.
5. Sarah Dening, a psycho therapist of UK, began her career by studying for a degree in Philosophy at London University and subsequently went on to work in film production, PR and then to run an art gallery. In the early 1980's, she set up the first public floatation tank facility in the UK whilst working towards becoming a Jungian psychotherapist. Many people had extraordinary experiences whilst floating including being reunited with a long-dead father and meeting an angel! For the last eighteen years she had been busy developing therapy practices in London and York. Dream work is an important aspect of Jungian therapy and she had worked with hundreds of clients, helping them to understand how their dreams can further their personal development. For nine years she had written a weekly national newspaper column interpreting readers' dreams in the *Daily Mail,* the *Daily Express* and, lately, in the *Daily Mirror.* She died in August 2007 with cancer. She wrote several books like *Healing Dreams, The Everyday I Ching, Dreams made Easy, The Mythology of Sex,* etc.
6. Dening, Sarah, *The Mythology of Sex*, Batsford Ltd, 5 Nov. 1996.
7. Sandars, N. K. (Translators): *The Epic of Gilgamesh*, Penguin, 1960.
8. Marling, Roderick W., *Vamacara Tantra*, KamaKala Publications, Portland, Oregon, 1997
9. Sandars, N. K. (Translators), opcit., p. 86
10. Dening, Sarah, op.cit.

9 Creativity and Sexuality

Sexuality may well be the most rewarding bliss of all possible experiences that life can offer between two people passionately attracted to each other. The union it produces between men and women in love is so close and so complete that two finite individuals can interrelate almost as if they were one indivisible beings. It involves not only physical but also psychological, spiritual, and somehow anthropological and social aspects. It is related to reproduction.

But because it does involve reproduction and transfer of genes, society has always tried to grip it under its control, denying any need of its other aspects. Even anthropological theories are denied by the social gurus. Society or religion (I am unable to differentiate them) articulates its own definition of sex as all sexual activity ought to be potentially reproductive, that marriage must last forever, and that women must be subject to men.[1]

'Dharma' in Hinduism is different from the Western concept of religion. It is a code related to moral nature. There is a very negligible difference between this 'dharma' and 'spiritualism' whereas in the Western concept, 'religion' and 'spiritualism' are two different concepts. So society or religion always plays a role to suppress the sexuality, and as the patriarchal dominance is more on these fields, questions about the morality and the politics of sex are usually considered in isolation from issues about gender and erotic sex.

But in spiritualism, it is related to an individual's understanding for salvation and freedom. For Hindu spiritualism, sexuality is represented as 'kama'. It is one of the four necessities, four aims of life: *Dharma*, *Artha* (material goods), *Kama* and *Moksha* (liberation from the cycle of death and rebirth).

Kama is defined as the enjoyment of appropriate objects by the five senses of hearing, feeling, seeing, tasting and smelling, assisted by the mind together with the soul. The ingredient in this is a peculiar contact between the organ of sense and its object, and the consciousness of pleasure which arises from that contact. This is called *Kama*. In Hindu spiritualism, *Kama* is not at all a 'prohibited' subject or we don't find any 'male dominancy' there. Taking the lovers' longing for reunion as a metaphor for the soul's longing for union with the divine makes sexuality more acceptable in 'Sufism.' And in a later period, 'Hindu Bhaktism' by Sri Chaitanya also adopted this idea easily. But in Western philosophy, the natural and the universal are sharply divided—like heaven and earth. The division of tasks between heaven and earth, suffering on earth and happiness beyond, is part and parcel of Western culture and its philosophy, religion and mythology. Westerners tend to see the sensuous world around us as false or illusory and the world 'beyond' as real. But in Hindu spiritualism, when you are in your sexual desire, you might sense complete presence in your sensuous world, a perfect moment which is spiritual, natural and carnal all at once.

Professor David Lee Miller, a noted scholar of English Renaissance Literature, currently Professor of English and Comparative Literature at the University of South Carolina at Columbia, tries to define creativity as the "feeling" of pure experience vital to a realistic grasp of life with the 'sensuous world' (Miller named it 'as-in-the-whole-Earth'). Plato first refused this 'sensuous world' and under his influence, Western thought has been dominated by a model (paradigm) of neglecting this knowledge and of value in experience. But Miller, in his book, tries to establish that creativity is of the whole Earth (or we can say 'sensuous world') rather than being limited to particular aspects.[2]

It is the philosophy of sexuality in Hindu spiritualism that made Kalidasa and Jaydeva write two great masterpieces: *Kumara Sambhava* (*Kalidasa*, fourth century B.C.) and *Gita Govinda* (*Jaydeva*, twelfth century A.D.). These works depict lovers in separation and union; in longing and abandonment, and have been portrayed in thousands of exquisite miniature paintings in India.

Kumara Sambhava is about the begetting of Kartikeya, the god of war, who was the son of Shiva and Pârvati, and depicts the monogamous form of sexuality. In contrast, the erotic love of Radha and Krishna in *Gita Govinda* is not limited to the love of only two persons, but is extended to the 1,600 women known as 'gopis.' Unlike in *Kumara Sambhava*, the love of Radha and Krishna was not at all a monogamous example as Radha never was the wife of Krishna and the 'gopis' were also well-connected with the god 'Lord Krishna' in sexual desire and lovemaking.

We can say the love of Krishna was polyamorous, and was more an evocation and elaboration of passionate love or an attempt to capture the exciting, fleeting moments of the senses. It could also be an evocation of the baffling ways in which love's pleasures and pains were felt before retrospective recollection, trying to regain a lost control over emotional life. This is why this love story grips our imagination every time we encounter the animated expressions, flashing eyes, and sinuous movements of a dancer, who as Radha, expresses her anger at Krishna's infidelities or who as Krishna, begs forgiveness for his irresponsible dalliance.

Gita Govinda was the first of its kind to be included in the ritual service of the temple of Lord Jagannath at Puri, one of the four most sacred pilgrimage places of Hinduism. So, as the concept of Brahmacharya (suppression of sexual desire) exists, so also exists the concept of spiritual sexism in every authentic entity in this Eastern religion. But the fundamentalists always try to prohibit sex though, no doubt, we are the product of sexuality and our mind characterises what it experiences, which has a great influence on how our mind perceives the creative process. This creative process, as an inherent sexuality, is always enhanced when we are in sexual desire or find ourselves in the grip of sexuality.

The writing process is a sexual process. When a writer wants to expose a physical life or an energetic life, a creative tension and a flow of energy is generated in the creative process. This creative tension, can be experienced as a sexual tension and the flow of energy creates life or describes a new life. Religion or society never cares for any artistic sensibility as Plato's domination, and so this inherent sexual influence over creativity has also always been denied by our sexual gurus. So, we find there are descriptions of fetishism, voyeurism, exhibitionism in the writings after the Second World War. We also find that our writers/artists/musicians always have an inclination towards their sexual orientation and sexual behaviour, and we encounter how much sexual desire they have.

We find Christina Rossetti, George Eliot, Mary Wollstonecraft, Willa Cather, Emily Dickinson, Sarah Orne Jewett, A. E. Housman, T. S. Eliot, Federico García Lorca, Charlotte Mew, Viscountess Rhondda, Cicely Hamilton, Elizabeth Robins,Virginia Woolf and Simone de Beauvoire were either homosexual or bisexual. In contrast, very few of Indian writers have had the courage to admit such truth but Amrita Pritam, Maitreyi Pushpa, Kamala Das, Harivanshrai Vachchan, and Rajendra Yadav are among them.

Still, Asian and African writers have not shown any admissible indication to point out their sexual inheritance in their writings, though their culture is more open to nature than

Western cultures. This is a peculiar situation of contradiction and one which we cannot pass up.

References

1. Aquinas, Thomas, *On the Truth of the Catholic Faith*, Book 3 "Providence," Trans. Vernon J. Bourke, Doubleday, New York, 1967.
2. Miller, David Lee, *Philosophy of Creativity*, Peter Lang Publishing Inc., New York, 1990.

10 Being Feminine: A Matter of Socialisation or Biology?

In one of my recently published interviews in *Muse India*,[1] I stated that I differed from Simon de Beauvoir in her 'Other' theory where she says, "one is not born but rather, becomes a woman." I further stated that I think a woman is born as a woman.

There are inherent physical, behavioraul, emotional and psychological differences between men and women, and we affirm and celebrate these differences as wonderful and complementary. These differences do not evidence the superiority of one sex over the other, but rather serve to show that each sex is complemented and made stronger by the presence of the other. As a different unit, similar to man, the female mass has its right for equity as well.

Such a statement by me surprised some of my scholar friends—how could I state this when it was known to me that according to social anthropology, gender is more a societal than a biological phenomenon? This article aims to clarify my stand.

I started the first article of this book with "My Bicycle and Me," where I wrote of my experiences of childhood. As my father had an obsession for a male child, he wanted to see me as a boy and, therefore, I was dressed as a boy; my hair was cut like a boy's; and I used to play boyish games with boys instead of girlish games with girls. In my second blogging, I mentioned my Portuguese friend's query, where he asked whether this had any impact on my sexuality in later life. It is clear that these cross-gender activities did not make any difference in my later life, and I grew up normally as a woman.

When I studied more about gender theories, especially in anthropology, I found that the anthropologists tried to confirm that gender is not innate but is based upon social and cultural conditions; my mind did not accept the theory so easily. Margaret Mead, in her anthropological study in 1935, concluded that the differences in temperament between men and women were not a function of their biological differences, rather, they resulted from differences in socialisation and the cultural expectations held for each sex.[2] This is, I think, the earliest study that led to the conclusion that gender is more a social and cultural factor than a biological one. According to this study, it is the social environment of the child, such as parents and teachers, that shapes the gender identity of a child. A child learns what to wear (girls in frocks and boys in shirt-pants); how and what to play (dolls for girls and cars for boys); how to behave (passivity and dependence in girls and aggressiveness and independence in boys); and how to reciprocate (gender-wise thoughts, feelings or behaviour). And these learnings confirm an appropriate gender-wise appearance and behaviour, which leads to gender identity.

The sex/gender distinction seen as a set and unchangeable dichotomy does not help social scientists. They might have feared that "the set of sex/gender distinction serve to 'ground' a society's system of gender differences, [but] the ground seems in some ways to be less firm than what it is supporting."[3] Other social anthropologists like Moira Gatens, Henrietta Moore, Pat Caplan dismiss the idea of a biological domain separated from the social. Even Pat Caplan declared that "...sexuality, like gender, is socially constructed."[4]

From the discussion above, one can see that gender identities are grounded in ideas about sex, and cultural mechanisms create men and women. But we also have to remember that the biological sex is related to chromosomal sex, genitalia, assigned birth sex, or initial gender role which are rooted deeply in science, and somehow proved rather than hypothetically assumed. Humans have 23 pairs of chromosomes within each cell; 22 of these are alike in both males and females. But when we come to the twenty-third pair, the sexes are not the same. Every woman has in her cells two of what we call the 'X' chromosome. But a man has just one X and another Y chromosome. These sets of chromosomes are what make males and females different.[5]

The sex hormones—primarily estrogen and testosterone—have a significant impact on the behaviour of males and females. For example, why do boys typically like to play with cars and girls like to typically play with dolls? Social anthropologists think it is the impact of socialisation while biological science thinks it is the role of these sex hormones which differentiate the choice children make gender-wise. Biology says the sex-specific differences in the brain are located both in the primitive regions, and in the neocortex—the higher brain region that contains 70 per cent of the neurons in the central nervous system.

The neocortex is divided into two hemispheres joined by a 200-million fibre network called the corpus callosum. The left hemisphere controls language analysis and expression and body movements while the right hemisphere is responsible for spatial relationships, facial expressions, emotional stimuli and vocal intonations. Females use both their right and left hemisphere to process language in certain circumstances while males just use one hemisphere. Females also reach puberty two years earlier than boys, as per biological science, and this changes the way they process social and sexual information.

There are still some characteristics and feelings that I think social anthropologists rule out for the sake of their theory. What about the voice pitch? Males have harsh voices and females have soft voices. This is a biological characteristic, and it is related to gender. The crisis of infertility may create a serious trauma to a female, which a male cannot feel. This is a feeling innate with specific feminine gender, and it is more a psychological and biological than a social problem. The menopausal psycho syndromes are totally biological and not categorised with this social gender theory. Social anthropologists emphasise that we are all trying to pass as a gender which is decided by cultural systems, not our biological sex. But what happens in the cases of transsexuals who do not pass it? The operation does not make their bodies fully male or fully female. The genitals will not function as genuine genitals, and their chromosomes cannot be changed. Voice pitch and other physical characteristics might reveal their transsexualism.

Actually, the high level of testosterone in males drives them toward some specific masculine characteristics, while the lack of high levels of estrogen in women creates a natural, biological push in the direction of feminine characteristics. Each gender has different strengths and weaknesses; this does not mean that one sex is superior or inferior to another. Being feminine is a woman's birthright! It is always hard for me to understand why any woman would want to give up this cherished possession. I feel proud and adore my feminine dress, grooming, carriage, posture, voice and language.

I want to use an integrated analysis of oppression which means that both men and women are subjected to oppression and stereotypes, and that these oppressive experiences have a profound affect on beliefs and perceptions. I am against the patriarchy role model of society but it does not mean that I want to replace a matriarchal form of society in place of the existing patriarchal one. What I want is to develop equal mutual relationships of caring and support between all genders, and I want to focus on strengthening women in areas such as assertiveness, communication, relationships and self-esteem.

Above all, I feel myself more a writer than a feminist. As a writer, I feel more sensible and sincere to my feelings and as a feminist, I am more inclined towards my femininity. I just don't understand how people can be feminists and not realise that to be feminist, you must also not be racist, ableist, homophobic, etc. If you are feeling oppressed by a masculine world, then you should not be prejudiced and bigoted towards other oppressed groups either, whether they are a result of patriarchy or not.

I hope my stand has been further clarified.

References

1. Sahoo, Sarojini, Interview. *Muse India*, Issue 28, Nov-Dec 2009. <http://www.museindia.com/showcurrent17.asp?id=1477>
2. Mead, Margaret, *Sex and Temperament in Three Primitive Societies*, New York: Dell.
3. Shapiro, Judith, "Transsexualism: Reflections on the Persistence of Gender and the Mutability of Sex in Body Guards." *The Cultural Politics of Gender Ambiguity*, Eds. Epstein. J and Straub, K., 1991.
4. Caplan, Pat, *The Cultural Construction of Sexuality*, New York: Routledge, 1987.
5. Migeon, Barbara R., MD, "Why females are mosaics, x-chromosome inactivation, and sex differences in disease." *Gender Medicine*, Volume 4, Issue 2, June 2007, pp. 97-105.

11 The Historic Role of Gender in Language

In her book *The Myth of Mars and Venus*, Deborah Cameron, a professor of Language and Communication at Worcester College of the University of Oxford, and a leading expert in the field of language and gender studies, describes that the "men are from Mars, women are from Venus's position."[1]

Every language reflects the prejudices of the society in which it evolved, and as the patriarchal control over the society prevailed for a long time, the language has also been organised with male-centric views. So, in many languages, we find there are multi-gender systems similar to biological differences of nature. In most of the languages (except Japanese), the nouns and pronouns either have 'masculine' or 'feminine' gender. In English, there is also a third gender known as 'neuter.' But in Hebrew, Greek, German, Spanish, French, and Portuguese and in Indian languages like Hindi, there are only two genders, and the prepositions or verbs have been modified according to the gender of the subject.

In comparison to these languages, my own language, Oriya, has gender-neutral characteristics. Though like English, in Oriya, there are three genders, but the variation is that its pronouns have no gender, and unlike Hindi, its verbs and prepositions are not modified according to the subject. Many Indian languages besides Oriya, like Tamil, Assamese and Bengali, have also gender-free pronouns.

This type of characteristic can also be seen in Persian, Finnish, Estonian, Hungarian, Basque, Japanese, Korean, Indonesian, Quechuan, Filipino and Tagalog. In some ways, the Chinese language can be marked as gender-neutral unless it contains a root for "man" or "woman."

For example, the word for doctor is *yīshēng* and can only be made gender-specific by adding the root for "male" or "female" in front of it. Thus, to specify a male doctor, one would need to say *nányīshēng*. Under normal circumstances both male and female doctors would simply be referred to as *yīshēng*.

The Pronoun Problem

In English, if the gender of a subject is not known, then often, the 'masculine gender' is used. For example: *When a student comes into the room, he should pick up a handout.* Here 'student' is a gender-neutral subject but a masculine gender 'he' is used for the pronouns. Like in Hindi, if anyone is coming, we say: *Koi ata hai.* Here the verb 'ata hai' is modified according to masculine gender whereas the gender of the subject (*Koi*: Anyone) is not known. In Oriya, we have no such baffling situation. Here *Kehi asuchhi* does not cite the gender of the subject. But in most of the languages, this gives feminists a good reason to think that this 'male dominance' contributes to making women invisible from grammar. The generic use of masculine pronouns, in referring to persons of unspecified gender, is also termed by the feminist thinkers as 'sexist' norm of language.

In English the pronouns are highly gender-concerned. But how will they be treated when the gender of the pronoun is not known? Feminists have advised us to use singular 'they' instead of using 'he' or 'she.' For example, we can say, *When a student comes into the room, they should pick up a handout.* The *Chicago Manual of Style* (abbreviated in writing as *CMS* or *CMOS*, or verbally as *Chicago*) is a style guide for American

English published since 1906 by the University of Chicago Press. The *CMS*, in its 13th edition, strongly reviewed this attempt of using singular 'they', and wrote: "Non-traditional gimmicks to avoid the generic masculine (by using he/she or s/he, for example) or to use 'they' as a kind of singular pronoun. Either way, credibility is lost with some readers."[2] But later in its 14th edition, the manual revised its stance and recommended: "The 'revival' of the singular use of 'they' and 'their,' citing its venerable use by such writers as Addison, Austin, Chesterfield, Fielding, Ruskin, Scott and Shakespeare."[3] The 15th Edition deals specifically with gender bias and nowhere does it mention the writers stuff. So they changed it again—proves it's a hot topic!

The Gendered Nouns Problem

Some feminists also find the use of some terms like Chairman, Fireman, Policeman, Mailman, Fisherman, Businessman, Milkman, Spokesman, Gunman, Mankind and Brotherhood objectionable as the words reinforce the idea that men are more powerful and have higher priority over women. Women's femininity becomes invisible when they accept being categorised in male gender-biased terms. It also means that women are only being recognised when classified in a masculine group. During the nineteenth century, attempts were made to make a feminine term for these masculine job-specific terms. This produced words like 'doctress' and 'professoress,' and even 'lawyeress,' all of which have fallen out of use; though waitress, stewardess and actress are in contemporary use for some speakers.

Janice Moulton first marked her objection on the use of 'Lady Doctor', 'Lady Typist', 'Lady Supervisor' as these jobs are meant for men, whose use has been extended to cover both men and women. She thinks that these norms are highly insulting for a woman, and a number of new words are also recommended, such as: chairperson, spokesperson, firefighter, mailcarrier, etc., as substitutes for the "sexist" words in common use.[4] Another common gendered expression, found particularly in informal speech and writing, is "you guys." This expression is used to refer to groups of men, groups of women, and groups that include both men and women. But "a guy" (singular) is definitely a man, not a woman, and that most men would not feel included in the expression "you gals" or "you girls." Similarly, the way the words Mr., Miss and Mrs. are used also make the feminists annoyed because "Mr." can refer to any man, regardless of his marital status while women are defined by their relationship to men (by whether they are married or not). A feminists solution to this problem is to use "Ms." (which doesn't indicate marital status) to refer to women.

Feminists hope that by means of such reforms in the universities, the language of all society might gradually be reformed, and that by means of such a reform in the language, the consciousness of people would be rendered more favourable to feminist ideas. But they oppose the job-specific terms when used to define the gender-specific status of the job holder. In India, nobody would ever call Mrs. Indira Gandhi as "Lady Prime Minister" or Ms. Pratibha Patil as "Lady President." But these words in Hindi or other languages have been treated as 'masculine.' Still now in India, these maleness of norms are not being identified by any feminists or any intellectuals.

But in Western linguistics, the scholars and feminists are more concerned about these 'maleness' of language. An increasing number of women are calling themselves actors rather than actresses, especially in the live theatre. The Screen Actors Guild of America (SAG) annually gives out awards for "Best Male Actor" and "Best Female Actor."

When my first novel was translated into Bengali and was published from Bangladesh, *Pratham Alo*, a leading daily of that country, reviewed that novel. The reviewer of that book cited me as a 'Lekhika' (woman writer) in his review, and the translator of that book, Morshed Shafiul Hassan, got irritated with the use of such a gender-biased term for me

The Patriarchal Problem in the *Bible*

Though Semitic religions are more male-centric (here God is always masculine), it is in the liberal Christian mind that attempts have been made by the churches to make a non-sexist, generic, and gender-neutral version of the *Bible*. The earliest example of such an effort was the *Inclusive Language Lectionary* published by the National Council of Churches in 1983. This new *Bible* excluded 1 Corinthians 11:3-16, 1 Corinthians 14:34-35, Ephesians 5:22-24, Colossians 3:18, 1 Timothy 2:11-15, and 1 Peter 3:1-6. In 1990, the excluded portions were also adapted into the new version of that *Bible*.[5] It did not, however, substitute gender-neutral language in reference to God, and it did not incorporate many of the misinterpretations proposed by feminists. And in doing so, it did not satisfy many liberals.

The American Bible Society published an abridged version of the *New Testament* in 1991 and then a complete version of the *Bible* in 1995. In that edition, while they did not use gender-neutral language for God, in Genesis 2:18, Eve is called not a "helper" but a "partner" of Adam.[6]

In another example, the Greek text of Matthew 16:24 states literally, "If anyone wants to follow me, he must deny himself and take up his cross and follow me." The *Contemporary English Version* shifts to a form which is still accurate and at the same time, more effective in English: "If any of you want to be my followers, you must forget about yourself. You must take up your cross and follow me."[7]

Later in 1994, a group of liberal Roman Catholics published *The Inclusive New Testament,* and the next year liberal Protestants published a similar version of *The New Testament and Psalms: An Inclusive Version*.[8] Both these versions featured gender-neutral language for God along with many other politically-correct alterations designed to combat racism, homophobia, ageism, etc. The liberties taken with the text of scripture in these versions were however so blatant, that they were met with resis ance in the popular press.

Up until 2004, 18 versions of the *Bible* had been published in non-sexist, gender-neutral generic language.[9]

Solving the Problem

In 1999, The United Nations Educational, Scientific and Cultural Organisation (UNESCO) issued guidelines for eliminating sexist stereotypes and language in common writing.[10] Gender-neutral language has gained support from most major textbook publishers, and from professional and academic groups such as the American Psychological Association and the Associated Press. Today, many law journals, psychology journals, and literature journals do not print articles or papers that use gender-inclusive language.

But in India, there is no debate so far insisting on gender-neutral language. This is due to lack of gender discrimination, consciousness and awareness. So while some progress has been made, there remains much room for improvement and development.

References

1. Cameron, Deborah, *The Myth of Mars and Venus: Do Men and Women Really Speak Different Languages?* Oxford University Press, USA, 2009.
2. *Chicago Manual of Style*, Chicago: University of Chicago Press, 13th edition, (1983), p. 233.
3. *Chicago Manual of Style*, op.cit., 14th edition (1993), p. 76-77.
4. Moulton, J., "The Myth of the Neutral 'Man'", *Sexist Language*, Ed. M. Vetterling-Braggin, Totowa. NJ: Littlefield and Adams, (1981), pp. 100–115.
5. Gold, Victor Roland, et al., *An Inclusive Language Lectionary*, 3 vols, Philadelphia: Westminster Press, 1983, 1984, 1985.

6. *The Contemporary English Version* (CEV), New York: American Bible Society, (1991, 1995).
7. Ibid., Matthew 16:24.
8. Gold, Victor Roland, Hoyt, Jr. Thomas L., Ringe, Sharon H., Thistlethwaite, Susan Brooks, Throckmorton, Jr. Burton H., Withers, Barbara A., *The New Testament and Psalms: An Inclusive Version*, Oxford University Press, USA (1995).
9. Marlowe, Michael D., *The Gender-Neutral Language Controversy.* (2001. revised January 2005) < http://www.bible-researcher. com/ inclusive.html>
10. *Guidelines on Gender Neutral Language.* <http://portal.unesco.org/es/ ev.php URL_ID=11489&URL_DO=DO_TOPIC&URL_ SECTION=201.html>

12 The Myth of Mars and Venus

Deborah Cameron, a professor of Language and Communication at Worcester College of the University or Oxford and a leading expert in the field of language and gender studies, wrote a book entitled *The Myth of Mars and Venus*[1] in which she describes that men are from Mars, women are from Venus's position, and reveals that differences between men and women are an issue of culture, not a fundamental difference in our chromosomal make-up. I borrowed this title from her book.

Away from the demands of feminists for the same status in language, some social linguistic scholars think the language of men and women differ in their speech patterns.

Women usually speak in a softer voice using pitch and inflection to emphasize points. They sound more emotional in speech. They use approximately five tones when talking, and interrupt others less and allow more interruptions. They disclose more personal information about themselves, and make more indirect accusations. They use "why," which sounds like nagging (i.e., "Why don't you ever call?"). They make more indirect statements, use more intensifiers such as "few", "so", "really", "much", "quite", make more tentative statements and use "tag endings" or upward inflections which make statements sound like questions (i.e., "It's a nice day, isn't it?"). They use more conjunctions when changing topics (i.e., "and", "but", "however") and ask more questions to stimulate conversations. They tend to establish more business relationships through discussing their personal life.

On the other hand, men speak in a louder voice using loudness to emphasize points. They sound more monotonous in speech. They use approximately three tones when talking and interrupt others more and allow fewer interruptions. They disclose less personal information about themselves; they make direct accusations (i.e., "You don't call"). They make more direct statements and "beat around the bush" less often, use less intensifiers, and make more declarative statements (i.e., "It's a nice day."). They use more interjections when changing topics (i.e., "Hey!", "Oh", "Listen!") and ask fewer questions to stimulate conversation. They rarely discuss their personal life in business.

In 1975, for the first time, the known grammarian Robin Lakoff claimed that there is a typical female language, very different from that of men, marked by the use of certain linguistic features such as hedging devices, tag questions, intensifiers and qualifiers, so-called "trivial lexis," "empty" adjectives, and rising intonation on declaratives. Specifically, the male use of language was considered the norm, and women's language was deviant from that norm, and thus being regarded as inferior to that of men.[2]

To justify his own statement, Lakoff put forward a "dominance approach" theory, according to which the difference in language between men and women is a consequence of male dominance and female subordination. In this view, women are a suppressed minority group.

But another group (supported by Jenifer Coates[3] (1986) and Deborah Tannen[4] (1990), on the other hand, believe that men and women belong to different subcultures, and that any linguistic differences can be attributed to cultural differences. They argued that men and women communicate differently (and women do it better) because of the way their brains are wired. The female brain excels in verbal tasks whereas the male brain is better adapted to visual-spatial and mathematical tasks. Women like to talk; men prefer action to words.

Claire Damken Brown and Audrey Nelson narrate in their recently published book[5] (2009) how men and women act in ingrained styles learned from birth and deeply embedded in the workplace structure. According to the authors, women tend to write long e-messages, which express support, and are more personal and emotive, while men are to the point with precise orders. They point out the following gender differences in their book:

1. Women play the role of "office mother" offering to lend a sympathetic ear.
2. Men play devil's advocate and act in a challenging way.
3. Women make the effort to laugh at jokes and make colleagues feel good about themselves.
4. Men are more likely to be the joke teller.
5. Women act in a passive manner, letting colleagues talk over them and interrupt.

In my opinion though, both the theories are somehow nearer to the truth. I strongly believe that men and women are coming from a different subculture and not only are they different in biological manner, but they are also different with their psycho-socio backgrounds. This is due to the way boys and girls are raised linguistically. Janet Holmes claimed that women often use empty phrases, like, I think or you know, because they are not committed to what they are saying and that they can be used to soften or mitigate utterances in order not to hurt the addressee's feelings.[6]

Women's expressions are mainly an interpretation of women's ideas and their surroundings, and I think they differ from men's harshness. The myth of Mars and Venus is no exception to that rule. But I don't find anything harassing if females are considered different. It is to be remembered that the world is built with two complimentary powers and male-female differences today did not exist in the same communities in early periods. It is the patriarchal society which makes its dominance over the feminine world. Those who are saying about the brain mapping, to prove that the female is a weaker sex, has itself become a dogma, treated not as a hypothesis to be investigated or as a claim to be adjudicated, but as an unquestioned article of faith.

References

1. Cameron, Deborah. *The Myth of Mars and Venus: Do Men and Women Really Speak Different Languages?* Oxford University Press, USA, 2009.
2. Lakoff, R. *Language and Women's Place*, New York: Harper & Row, 1975.
3. Coates, Jennifer, *Men, Women and Language*, London: Longman, 1996.
4. Tannen, Deborah, *You Just Don't Understand: Women and Men in Conversation*, New York: Ballentine Books, 1990.
5. Brown, Claire Damken and Nelson, Audrey, *Code Switching: How to Talk So Men Will Listen*, Alpha Books, 2009.
6. Holmes, J., "Women's Talk in Public Contexts", *Discourse and Society*, Vol..3, issue number 2, 1992, p.131-150.

13 All For One But Maybe Not One For All

'Manuvad' has become a hot topic in Indian politics today. The orthodox RSS and its feeding political party like BJP are more likely advocating the 'ism,' whereas the 'dalit political parties' like BSP have raised their voices against that inhuman religious code. Manuvad, based on *Manu Samhita*[1] or *Manu Smriti* as the 'social code,' presents itself as a discourse given by the sage Manu to a group of seers, or rishis, who beseeched him to tell them the "law of all the social classes (1.2)." Manu became the standard point of reference for all future *Dharmashastras* that followed it. However, there are still some fallacies in the Hindu mind regarding *Manu Smriti* or *Manu Samhita.*

Fallacies and Facts

Fallacy: Manu Samhita is a part of Vedic Scriptures.

Fact: The Vedic period stretched from the second and first millennia BCE continuing up to the sixth century BCE based on literary evidence. Mahavira and Buddha arrived in around sixth century BCE and they both counter-attacked Vedic concepts on social and spiritual grounds. These two preachers never claimed themselves as God and they are also considered as the path finders of Hinduism. Buddhism became a separate religion when it came to China. The dominance of Buddha and Mahavira over Hinduism continued up to Maurya Empire (from ca. 320 BCE). And this period also was treated as the golden age, the classical age of Sanskrit literature, and the

Middle kingdoms of India. After the breakdown óf the Maurya and Sunga empires, there was a period of uncertainty that led to renewed interest in traditional social norms and the Brahmanical religion, which suffered during Buddhist and Jainist rule, tried to revive it again. The *Manu Smriti* or *Manu Samhita* was written at that time, and critics find contradictions in concept, especially when the scriptures try to state the position of women in society.

Certain verses of *Manu Samhita* (e.g. III - 55, 56, 57, 59, 62) glorify the position of women, while other verses (e.g. IX-3, 17) seem to attack the position and freedom women have. Certain interpretations of verses IX-18 claim that it discourages women from reading Vedic scriptures. But verse II-240, however, allows women to read Vedic scriptures. Similar contradictory phrases are encountered in relation to child marriage in verses IX-94 and IX-90.

It is also doubtful that the scriptures were written by a single person and were probably written by many. Some scriptures in the *Samhita* are so contradictory that the founder of Arya Samaj, Swami Dayanand Saraswati, a noteworthy nineteenth-century campaigner for women's rights, cites Manu's laws hundreds of times in his writings. In his opinion, verses highly critical of women and the lower classes (sudras) are not Vedic at all but interpolations introduced later by the corrupted Brahminical class. Another scholar, Dr. Surendra Kumar, claims that out of a total of 2,685 verses in the current *Manu Smriti*, only 1,214 are authentic or can be confirmed by the *Vedas*; the other 1,471 are purported to be interpolations.

Fallacy: It is believed that the text is the earliest and foremost, and the only law created by Manu, whose status is like Moses in Greco-Semitic religions.

Fact: Manu's time period is 200 B.C.E to 200 A.C.E, while Moses died in about Feb. Mar. 1271 BCE.[2] The Greco-Semitic religion started with Moses, but Manu is much more younger to the History of Hinduism. Secondly, the *Manu Samhita* is not the only source of Hindu laws as it is claimed. There is also the Laws of Yājñavalkya in the Hindu religion. Besides these two authors, Āpastamba, Gautama, Baudhāyana and Vasishtha are some writers who were well versed in *Dharmashastra*, a primarily Hindu text which refers to religious and legal duty.

Fallacy: The text claims that Bhrigu was a student of Manu, to whom he (Manu) taught these lessons.

Fact: Actually Bhrigu was a saint of the Vedic period in around 3000 B.C.E.[3]

Hence it is mere or virtual imagination or a deliberately wrong quoted misrepresentation that Manu taught his *Samhita* to Bhrigu.

Fallacy: The British colonial rulers and contemporary conservative Hindu radicals claim that the *Manu Samhita* is followed universally by Hindus and is a common code for Hindu religion.

Fact: The *Manu Samhita* was never followed by Hindus unanimously. In earlier days, the Vaishnavaites, the Shaivas and the Smartas never followed this text. In modern times, modern liberals, Hindu reformists, Dalit advocates, feminists, Marxists are the firebrand critics of this *Samhita.* It is only the British ruler, who paid importance to *Manu Samhita* to prepare codes of law for the natives. In 1794, Sir William Jones published the English translation of the *Samhita* to help the British ruler, and it was propagated as the only Hindu code by the British administration.

What *Manu Samhita* Advised

The Laws of Manu has 2,694 stanzas in 12 chapters. The inhuman code of Manu divides Hindus into four varnas: Brahmin, Kshatriya, Vaishya and Shudra. According to Manu, the supreme creator Brahma gave birth to the Brahmins from his mouth; the Kshatriyas from his shoulders; the Vaishyas from his thighs; and the Shudras from his feet (Manu's code I-31.)

Let the first part of a Brahmin's name denote something auspicious; a Kshatriya's be connected with power; and a Vaishya's with wealth; but a Shudra's, express something contemptible (Manu II. 31.)

Let the second part of a Brahmin's name be a word implying happiness; of a Kshatriya's, a word implying protection; a Vaishya's, a term expressive of thriving; a Shudra's, an expression denoting service (Manu II. 32).

A Shudra is unfit to receive education. The upper varnas should not impart education or give advice to a Shudra. It is not necessary that the Shudra should know the laws and codes and hence need not be taught. Violators will go to *asamrita* hell (Manu IV-78 to 81). One must never read the *Vedas* in the presence of the Shudras (Manu IV. 99). He who instructs Shudra pupils and he whose teacher is a Shudra shall become disqualified from being invited to a *shradha* (Manu III. 156).

A Brahmin who is only a Brahmin by decent, i.e., one who has neither studied nor performed any other act required by the *Vedas* may, at the king's pleasure, interpret the law to him, i.e., act as the judge, but never a Shudra, however learned he may be (Manu VIII. 20). Any Brahmin, who enslaves or tries to enslave a Brahmin, is liable for a penalty of no less than 600 PANAS. A Brahmin can order a Shudra to serve him without any remuneration because the Shudra is created by Brahma to serve the Brahmins. Even if a Brahmin frees a Shudra from slavery, the Shudra continues to be a slave as he is created for slavery. Nobody has the right to free him (Manu VIII-50,56 and 59). A Shudra who insults a twice–born man (i.e. a Brahmin) with gross invectives shall have his tongue cut out for he is of low origin (Manu VIII. 270). If he mentions the names and castes of the (twice-born) wit contumely, an iron nail, ten fingers long, shall be thrust red hot into his mouth (Manu VIII. 271). If a Shudra arrogantly presumes to preach religion to Brahmins, the king shall order burning oil to be poured in his (Shudra's) mouth and ears (Manu VIII. 272). No

Shudra should have property of his own; he should have nothing of his own. The existence of a wealthy Shudra is bad for the Brahmins. A Brahman may take possession of the goods of a Shudra (ManuVIII-417 & X129). No superfluous collection of wealth must be made by a Shudra, even though he has the power to make it, since a servile man, who has amassed riches, becomes proud, and, by his insolence or neglect, gives pain to Brahmins (Manu X. 129).

Manu's attitude was not only wild and inhuman for the Shudras. He possessed more furious ideas about women. His code describes:

> In childhood, a female must be subject to her father; in youth to her husband; then to her sons. A woman must never be independent. There is no God on earth for a woman than her husband.... She must on the death of her husband allow herself to be burnt alive on the same funeral pyre, that everyone will praise her virtue.

According to Manu, all women are liars, corrupt, greedy, and unvirtuous (Manu II 1). It is the nature of women to seduce men in this (world); the wise are never unguarded in the company of males (Manu II. 213). Killing of a woman, a Shudra, or an atheist is not sinful. Women are an embodiment of the worst desires, hatred, deceit, jealousy and bad character. Women should never be given freedom (Manu IX. 17 and V. 47, 147). One should not sit in a lonely place with one's mother, sister, or daughter, for the senses are powerful and master even a learned man (Manu II. 215). A Brahmin male by virtue of his birth becomes the first husband of all women in the universe (Manu III. 14). Though destitute or virtuous, or seeking pleasure elsewhere, or devoid of good qualities, yet a husband must be constantly worshipped as a god by a faithful wife (Manu V. 154). At her pleasure, let her (i.e. widow) enunciate her body by living voluntarily on pure flowers, roots and fruits, but let her not when her lord is deceased, even pronounce the name of another man (Manu V. 157). A woman must always maintain her virtue and surrender her body to her husband only, even if she is married off to an ugly person or even a leper (Manu IX. 14). Women have no right to study the *Vedas.* That is why their *Sanskars* are performed without *Veda Mantras.* Women have no knowledge of religion because they have no right to know the *Vedas.* The uttering of *Veda Mantras*, they are as unclean as untruth is (Manu IX. 18). None of the acts of women can be taken as good and reasonable (Manu X.4). A woman shall not perform the daily sacrifices prescribed by the *Vedas.* If she does it, she will go to hell (Manu XI. 36/37).

Manu Samhita's Utility in Recent Days

Actually the *Manu Samhita* lost its significance in a later period. The code was not accepted by the Hindus, the Shaivas, Smartas and Vaishnavaites created their own codes of law. During the colonial rule, Robert Clive and Lord Macaulay gave another incarnation of Manu, finding this code as a useful tool to divide and rule over the Hindus. They argued that the caste system, as prescribed by the *Manu Samhita*, developed a *de-facto* apartheid social system that was very easy to subjugate and rule.

Hinduism is a different and a broad 'platform' for all, which the colonial rulers could not understand. It is different from other religions. Buddhism, Jainism and Skhism are also considered as a part of Hinduism. It is the political scenario which barred Christianity or Islam to merge with Hinduism. Otherwise, these religions might be considered as a part of Hinduism. The "Dharma" of Hinduism or "Dhamma" of Buddhism is different from the term 'religion.' It may be a fact of history that the politics of a ruler is always to try to hide this truth from the people and to try to misguide them. But, it is 100 per cent true that this was not the original intention of the rishis and sages who actually produced the scriptures. In fact, there is constant reference in the Vedas to 'Bahujana Hitay' meaning the welfare of all people. Only in the medieval centuries, there was a lot of perversion, and the so-called lower castes were oppressed and feminine freedom was denied.

Never has the *Manu Samhita* been found acceptable in the Hindu mind. Even the modern Hindu mind practically does not want to follow this rule. It is also very notorious to say that all upper-caste Hindus are Manuvadi, as some dalit leaders often used to say in their public statements. They are the political parties who try to cash-in votes using the *Manu Samhita* as their currency. And perhaps this is where the Indian people are at the highest risk.

References

1. Jones, Sir William, Trans, *Institutes of Hindu Law*, Calcutta: Sewell & Debrett, 1796. <http://books.google.com/books?id =4caNTgBa6oEC&printsec=frontcover&source=gbs v2 summary r&cad =0#v=onepage&q=&f=false
2. Jacobs, Joseph, et al., "Death of Moses", *Jewish Encyclopedia.com.* http://jewishencyclopedia.com/view.jsp? artid=830&letter=M&search= moses#2846
3. Vaidya, Ashok D. B. "Bhrigu-Samhita: An ancient manuscript with medical matters of interest." *Current science*, Vol. 81, No. 7, 10 October, 2001.

14 The Beauty Dilemma

That day, one of my younger colleagues wore a pair of earrings, which made her face bright and beautiful. She looked quite pretty and we, that is, all the female teachers, appreciated this. Meanwhile, one of our senior male colleagues made comments about her 'so provocative' get-up. "What is the difference between 'beautiful' and 'provocative?" I asked that older teacher. And he replied, "Whatever it may be argued, but a teacher should keep herself away from any fashion." I laughed and told him, "I wish Betty Friedan were here; she could see how similar her ideas are with yours." Certainly my old colleague doesn't know who Betty Friedan is, so he considered it as a compliment to him!

Betty Friedan (1921) was a leading figure in the second wave of the U.S. Women's Movement and is mostly known for her book *The Feminine Mystique*,[1] which is considered as a succeeding effort of Simone De Beauvoir's *The Second Sex*.[2] Simone's great comment, "One is not born, but rather, becomes a woman", influenced her successor feminists so much that the total attitude of second wave feminists changed. She wrote *The Second Sex* in 1949. In French, *Le Deuxième Sexe* was published. Jonathan Cape first translated it into English and it came to America in 1953. In that book, Simone wrote that patriarchy always attempts to trap a woman into an impossible ideal by denying the individuality and situation of all different kinds of women. Patriarchy tries to impose an authentic false aura of 'womanhood' in them.

In 1963, ten years after *The Second Sex* was published in America, Betty Friedan's *The Feminine Mystique* was published. In this book, she described the social pressures on women to be 'beautiful' as an example of a patriarchal society's conspiracy against them. She explained that to serve women as good consumers of the thousands of products and services, the fashion industry consciously manipulates its portrayal of women. Although her book focused primarily on advertising's images of women as housewives, in later periods, radical feminists focused on advertising's use of sexual implication and feminine attraction to sell products, and the term 'sex object' was coined and became part of the English-speaking vocabulary.

The advertising industry was blamed, and there were protests against the cosmetic and fashion industries. Women were asked by these feminists to give up cosmetics and fashions. In 1968, a group of women picketing the Miss America Pageant in Atlantic City tossed their bras in the garbage, getting instant media coverage and, hence, the term "bra-burners"[3] entered the media vocabulary as a pejorative for feminists.

Then came Naomi Wolf and Ariel Levy with their books *The Beauty Myth* [4](1991) and *Female Chauvinist Pigs: Women and the Rise of Raunch Culture*[5] (2005), respectively. Both the books are considered to be successors to *The Feminine Mystique*, where, like Friedan, the writers argue that to make a woman interested in fashion and beauty culture is purely political and also a part of the process to maintain the patriarchal system. Naomi Wolf argues, in *The Beauty Myth* that American culture's images of beauty—found on television, in advertisements, women's magazines, and pornography—are detrimental to women, and are a weapon used to make women feel badly about themselves. In Ariel Levy's book, *Female Chauvinist Pigs: Women and the Rise of Raunch Culture*, she states that there are two types of feminists: 'lipstick feminists' and 'loophole women.'

According to Levy, lipstick feminists believe, for example, that stripping is empowering and that putting on a show to attract men (be it through make-up, clothing, or girl-on-girl gyration) is not contrary to the goals and ideals of feminism. These feminists sometimes exaggerated in their essays by adding overstated and false facts. These can be observed from few excerpts of Wolf's book:

> A century ago, normal female activity, especially the kind that would lead women into power, was classified as ugly and sick. If a woman read too much, her uterus would 'atrophy.' If she kept on reading, her reproductive system would collapse and, according to the medical commentary of the day, 'we should have before us a repulsive and useless hybrid'...Participation in modernity, education and employment was portrayed as making Victorian women ill...Victorians protested women's higher education by fervidly imagining the damage it would do to their reproductive organs and it was taken for granted that 'the education of women would sterilise them' and make them sexually unattractive: 'When a women displays scientific interest, then there is something out of order in her sexuality.

Wolf was against the feminine idea of getting slim by just going on a diet to lose weight in order to make one's fitness in beauty competitions. She claimed this tendency may create diseases like anorexia and bulimia. These are eating disorders. Wolf falsified facts in her said book, quoting the American Anorexia and Bulimia Association [reports] that "anorexia and bulimia strike one million American women every year. Each year 150,000 American women die of anorexia." Later, Gloria Marie Steinem, a feminist journalist, quoted the same facts in her book *Revolution from Within*[6] (1992) which supported these facts. But after publication of *The Beauty Myth*, the president of the American Anorexia and Bulimia Association denied the fact. In a 1985 newsletter[7], the association hadn't referred to deaths at all, but rather to anorexia sufferers, a state prone to subjective assessment. In 1988, the National Center for Health

Statistics reported 67 deaths from anorexia, and its Division of Vital Statistics reported 54 deaths in 1991. The figures used by these feminists for anorexia deaths are 2,238 and 2,777 per cent greater than that found by any serious scientific source!

Many times Western feminists, especially the second wave feminists, adopted these fanatics, falsified, or wrong determinations to challenge the patriarchal hegemony of the "sex/gender system." Simone's ideas made the feminists of the second wave keep themselves away from the masculine world. They refused to make themselves instruments (objects) towards masculine sexual pleasure, and even kept themselves away from heterosexuality. We find the feminists of that time were either bisexual or lesbians. The result was that many women who generally supported feminism were not prepared to fully accept the ideological underpinnings proposed by these radicals and socialist feminists. Linda Scott, a pop singer feminist admits in her book *Fresh Lipstick: Redressing Fashion and Feminism*[8] that feminism had suffered a lot because of its views on beauty and fashion.

Fashion is a barometer of cultural changes. It not only embraces clothing, but also accessories, jewellery, hairstyles, beauty and body art. What we wear, and how and when we wear it provides others with a shorthand to subtly read the surface of a social situation. Fashion is a form of non-verbal communication to indicate occupation, rank, gender, sexual availability, locality, class, wealth and group affiliation. Fashion is a form of free speech. It is the best form of iconography that we have to express individual identity. Popular personalities are known to us by their fashion.

For example, Mahatma Gandhi's short 'dhoti,' bare body, round spectacles, and long stick are sufficient to make his iconography. Further, we can easily associate icons with Karl Marx for his thick beard, Abraham Lincoln for his attire, and Indira Gandhi for her short hair. In fact, cartoonists routinely use the individual fashion of a personality as a part of their iconography.

For centuries, the authority (state, society, or religion) tended to grip its control over individuals on the use of fashion. Emperor Napoleon stopped the import of English textiles, and he revived the local fabric industry so that fine fabrics like tulle and batiste could be made there. To make women buy more material, he forbade them to wear the same dress more than once to court. During the Emergency in 1970, Indira Gandhi imposed a ban against the wearing of 'bell-bottom pants' by girls and keeping long 'hippie hair' by boys. Police were authorised to cut the pants and hairs of the students. I remember my father bought two 'saris' for me, though I was not comfortable with this long-wear style. The orthodox semi-socio-political parties now run their schools in India, where they impose a dress code not only for students but also for teachers as well. In Orissa and in other states also, the government has imposed dress codes for students. In Judaism and Islam, they have a written dress code in their holy books. In many religions, though there are no written codes, a magnificent non-verbal practice has been traditionally continuing.

The authorities always show a reluctant attitude for any change in the system of fashion. Socially, there is a great difference between taboo and fashion. Every society prescribes fashions for different genders, and the modification in these items are considered as fashion, but the use of the other gender's item is called 'taboo.' Hence society considers cross-dressing as a taboo, not as a fashion.

Indian readers will remember that once the orthodox Muslim Mullahs raised their objection on the wearing of short pants to Sania Mirza, an international tennis player. Ironically, she was asked to wear traditional Muslim dresses while playing tennis.

But history shows us that with the change of time, these taboos too sometimes change with fashion. In the last few decades of the nineteenth century, when trousers were first introduced for women instead of traditional skirts, the *New York Times* pointed out the trend as "A Curious Disease" in its editorial and wrote: women in trousers needed treatment in "the best conducted hospitals for the insane."[9] But after the Second World War, trousers became the mass uniform for ladies. Trousers may have begun to be worn during the war as many women went to work in ammunitions and other factories there to help the war effort and due to the unavailability of men. In the early 1980s, fashion designers tried to create a groundswell of skirt-wearing men in the previously skirt-phobic regions of the West, but the fashion never caught on with the public. So, we can't say that the 'market' (which includes advertising) does not decide the trend of fashions but it is the consumer who decides what to adopt or what not to adopt.

Sometimes institutions or authorities introduce this cross-dressing as a new fashion to society. The woman empowerment policy of the Government in India made trouser and shirt as a mass uniform for the women members in the police and home guards. The leftist Maoist-Leninist Political Party, popularly known as Naxal in India, prepared their own comrades for guerilla warfare, and they introduced trousers and shirts for their women fighters. Nobody asked the authenticity or peculiarity of these fashions, or are these not counted as cross-dressing?

In the third wave or post-modern era of feminism, some feminists came forward with their avant-garde idea to save feminism in America. The long tradition of denying feminine mystique was again put on trial, and the issue of personal appearance has been used repeatedly as an instrument of power and control within the women's movement, reinforcing biases of class, education and ethnicity. These avant-garde feminists pointed out that people in every culture and throughout history have groomed and decorated themselves, and for a complex variety of reasons, not just sexual attraction.

The eighties saw a group of "American feminists" come forward to counter the ideas of *The Beauty Myth* and its followers. Lois Banner's *American Beauty* [10] (1983), Rita Freedman's *Beauty Bound* [11] (1985), and Valerie Steele's *Fashion and Eroticism*[12] (1985) were some landmarks, which opposed the radical and social feminists idea that beauty and fashion subjugate over the power of women. They argued that the use of fashion and beauty products evolved as a rejection of the Victorian prohibition on sensual expression, and that it was absurd to blame fashion, as such, for turning women into sexual objects, as men and women look differently and do different things. Rather than considering beauty products as symbols of oppression, these new feminists urged the pragmatic recognition that beauty is one of the few paths to power that women have whether they be producing or consuming. For example, nearly all the founders of major cosmetics companies in America were women: Elizabeth Arden, Helena Rubenstein, Estée Lauder, Dorothy Gray, and others.

In India, feminism does not have such variances in dimension as in America. Here, feminists still show their neutral attitude for fashion and beauty. Rather, the anti-feminists or misogyny attitudes try to get a control over feminine fashion and beauty culture. But there is a strange similarity in the attitude of Western social and radical feminists of the second wave and the patriarchal society of India as far as the sexual objectification of women is concerned. Both of them believe women have often been valued mainly for their physical attributes. Here in our country, the 'izzat' (prestige or pride) of a family means a lot, and it is always associated with the 'chastity' of female members of the family. If a boy falls in love with a girl, the boy's family does not have to care for the loss of their 'izzat,' but on the other hand, the girl's family feels they have lost their 'izzat,' when a daughter falls in love with a boy. So the 'authority' of a family often shows too much concern about the fashion, get-up and behaviour of the female members of their family. The restrictions are enforced and different behavioural codes are created. Though the 'head of the family' requires the female members of the family to obey that behavioural code, the male members of that same family may show excess affiliation towards the females of other families who are prone to fashion or beauty make-ups.

But the contradictory fact is, still 'beauty parlours' are brooding up in small to smaller urban areas and even in semi-urban villages. The tribal girls, who were supposed to adopt 'natural' get-up, are also showing their fascination for stylish haircuts or in using cosmetics. The 'fashion' is not restricted to any age group, and we can see all age groups (16-60) show their interest in beauty culture. Today, beauty parlours are not limited to just female customers; they have added male customers as well. Still reluctant attitudes have prevailed in society regarding feminine fashion.

Actually in our subcontinent, we are living in a great paradoxical confusion. The patriarchal restrictions differ with variance of caste, class, and even vary from region to region. In rural areas, the restrictions are more than in urban areas. In comparison to urban areas, those in the metro (big cities) areas are more liberal. The liberal attitudes again depend on literacy also. So, in such a mixed and confused state, it is difficult to generalise any statement. But above all, it is true that still in India, the grip of patriarchy is very much present and most masculine groups, irrespective of caste, creed, class, region or language, would not prefer to see that their 'izzats' (women in their families) are enjoying complete freedom like them.

References

1. Friedan, Betty, *The Feminine Mystique*, Penguin Book (reprint, 1972).
2. Beauvoire, Simone, Trans, H M Parshley, *The Second Sex*, Penguin (reprint edition, 1972).

3. Greenfieldboyce, Nell, "Pageant Protest Sparked Bra-Burning Myth," *npr: FIND A STATION.* September 5, 2008 < http://www.npr.org/templates/story/story.php?storyId=94240375>
4. Wolf, Naomi, *The Beauty Myth: How Images of Beauty Are Used Against Women,* Vintage. 1991.
5. Levy, Ariel. *Female Chauvinist Pigs: Women and the Rise of Raunch Culture.* Free Press, 2005
6. Steinem, Gloria, *Revolution from Within: A Book of Self-Esteem,* Little, Brown and Company, 1992.
7. Sommers, Christina Hoff, "Figuring out feminism - how feminists abuse statistical information to serve their political agenda - Cover Story", *National Review*, (USA) June 27, 1994.
8. Scott, Linda M., *Fresh Lipstick: Redressing Fashion and Feminism,* Palgrave Macmillan, 2004.
9. "Editorial", *The NY Times,* May 27, 1876, p.6.
10. Banner, Lois, *American Beauty*, Univ of Chicago Pr (T), 1984.
11. Freedman, Rita. *Beauty Bound*, Prentice Hall & IBD, 1985.
12. Steele, Valerie, *Fashion and Eroticism: Ideals of Feminine Beauty from the Victorian Era Through the Jazz Age*, Oxford University Press, USA, 1985.

15 Skin Colour among Indians—Is it Really a Question of Fairness?

Recently, Liz, one of my American readers, shared her feelings with me about India. She told me that some conversations with her friends baffled her and she would like to hear my answer. Liz's letter inspired me to write this article.

In her letter, she writes, "I was speaking with a girl from New Delhi about India, and the conversation turned to me complimenting Indians' many skin tones and undertones like, ginger snap, chocolate, cinnamon, gold or caramel, when she ruined the moment by saying, 'Well, most Indians aren't that dark...most are wheatish. Darker skin tones are mainly in the South.' Really??? Then she said more or less, that if North Indians are darker than wheatish they usually have a sun tan. The complexions that I described, I have seen on travel shows that went to various parts of India. mainly the North, like Rajasthan. So all this time most Indians aren't dark-skinned like I thought?"

Another girl, also a friend of the above, always attributed dark skin to "the climate." Like, 'They're dark because of the climate.' I mentioned to her how some Africans have black skin and she seriously asked 'because of the climate?' I've read of other Indians on *Sepia Mutiny* who attribute India's colour to caste and that caste was based on skin colour. That dark skin was from working outdoors and the upper caste 'stayed' light-skinned indoors. She then asked me, "Are Indians in denial that they're a dark-skinned race of people?"

In response, I told Liz that I am not at all interested in determining what skin colours Indians have. I have always believed that racism is bad wherever and in whatever form it takes. But it is also not a fact of any pride to show one's self-superiority on the basis of one's body colour. It is also not justified to use body colour as the basis of any creed or caste.

Racial Diversity in India

India has vast diverse racial and cultural origins. The exact origins of most Indian people are almost impossible to determine because of the large variety of races and cultures that have invaded and have been assimilated into the subcontinent. There are elements of three major racial groups: the Caucasoid, the Australoid, and the Mongoloid. All may be found in present-day India. But it is also debatable whether the people from southern India (the so-called Dravidians) belong to the Caucasoid group or not.

The languages related to these races are also different in origin. Assamese and Oriya are nearer to each other in dialect but differ in their racial origin; Oriyas are nearer to Caucasoid while Assamese are nearer to Mongoloid.

All tribal people do not belong to the Australoid groups, and in some parts of Eastern India, we find a mixed race of these groups which we may call as Sankara or mixed group (Sankara in Sanskrit means mixed varieties).

Common Myths about the Colour of Our Skin

The melanocytes in the epidermis are responsible for the intensity of skin colour. The number of melanocytes is the same in both fair- and dark-skinned people. The amount of melanin produced by the melanocytes is partly determined by genetics and partly determined by the environment. People living near the tropics have more melanin to protect them from the harsher rays of the sun. There are some myths with dark skin in the Indian mind, which have no scientific basis.

The first myth is that 'white skin' is linked with the Aryan race while 'black' skin is Dravidian and tribal. So people of the 'north' in India are fair and people of the 'south' are black. The 'brown-coloured' people are from the mixed races ('shankar') of Aryan with both Dravidian and Tribal. This is totally wrong. The theory of 'Aryan invasion' is still a debatable controversy and if the so-called 'Dravidians,' people from south, are 'dark coloured,' how then do we find most of the Bollywood south Indian film actresses with 'very fair skin?' How do people from Rajasthan and Maharashtra, Gujarat don't appear to be so 'fair?'

The second myth is 'white' people are from aristocratic and rich families whereas 'dark' people are from the labour class or are 'tribal.' This is also wrong. The tribal people of North-East India have 'pale' and 'fair' skin. I have encountered many 'dalit' girls in my surroundings with fair skin.

In South Asia, pale skin is considered as a social marker of aristocratic class allegiance. A peculiar idea in the *desi* mind still prevails that dark skin is associated with labour class people as some of Liz's friends told her. I think this notion has been a result of colonialism, as India was under British colonial rule for more than 200 years, and the British people kept themselves alien from the native people on this racial ground. In post-colonial India, the word "Saheb" (which was meant to call the "white" people) has been used for the upper-class people or bureaucrats as a mark of honour to them. I think, this racial skin preference has its roots in an historic background.

From Myth to Reality

I recently recollected a conversation in the staff common room of my college where I have been employed. This issue of skin colour came into sharp focus as I silently listened. A new person joined us as a laboratory assistant in physics. Finding him a bachelor, one of my colleagues, a lecturer in zoology, asked him what type of bride he would like. He replied, "Surely a fair skinned girl." The zoology lecturer again asked, "What if the girl has only fair skin and hasn't any sharp body features?" The newcomer replied, "I can manage. The fair skin has its own charm."

I was a silent listener there, as I didn't want to impose my feminist ideas there to continue a confronting argument. But the answers of that newcomer had embarrassed me for a while. In our 'matrimonial ads,' we often find 'looking for a fair, beautiful girl' is a common phrase from the prospective groom's side. I haven't read any ad asking for a 'fair skinned groom.'

To write this article, I searched for the 'business survey' of fairness cosmetics products, and found that there are at least 12 creams on the market from different companies claiming to make your skin fairer within seven days. The report indicated that their business leapfrogged from 384 crore in 1997-1998 to 558 crore in 1999-2000. And in six months between 2000 and 2001, sales reached up to 480 crore.[1]

Besides these fairness-out-of-a tube brands, there are also soaps and tales claiming to remove blemishes to give the users a smooth and glowing complexion. Their business turnover is not included here. These business houses have tried to trap their 'male consumers' by creating a 'fair-skinned consciousness' among boys. Recently, Bollywood mega-star Shahrukh Khan appeared in a television commercial offering a tin of skin-whitener to dark complexioned young boys who are unlucky with the ladies. The darker complected boy then suddenly attains popularity with women because apparently, the skin-whitener has lightened his complexion. It may seem amazing to Indian readers that in North America and other part of Europe, tanning has become a profitable industry, while in South Asia, people spend millions of dollars trying to make their skin darker.

There are numerous Hindu gods and goddesses who are dark or blue or dusky in appearance. Draupadi, a prominent character of the mythical epic *The Mahabharata*, was dark in appearance. She captivated and enamoured all the men of her era. Kings and princes were even ready to go into war for her. She had arranged for a *swayamvara* to choose her husband.

But today, Hindu parents of dark-complexioned sons always prefer fair brides. But the same parents lament that their dark-complexioned daughter is not getting a good husband due to her skin colour. What is most baffling is that we are ready to worship the dark-skinned gods and take their blessings but are not ready to accept a dark-skinned person as a life partner.

The Effects of Bollywood and Hollywood

The colour mania has also affected Bollywood filmmakers, and there we find they always make it a point to get a dark man to play the villain, the rapist, the goonda, and mafia man, only to be beaten up by fair-skinned heroes. The Bollywood movies and TV serials are also responsible for giving the idea among the masses that that dark-skinned girls don't have a chance of finding love. It is also a literary device common in books, plays and opera as well.

Meanwhile, in the United Kingdom, we see a black model Naomi Campbell establish herself as a supermodel, while in the United States, Angela Bassett, Alfre Woodard, Diahann Carroll, Halle Berry, Whoopi Goldberg, Kerry Washington, Thandi Newton, Jennifer Hudson, Rosario Dawson, Tracie Thomas, Queen Latifah, Jada Pinkett Smith, Regina King, Sharon Warren, Marianne Jean-Baptiste, Macy Gray, Lackawanna Blues and countless other black actresses from different generations have glowed in the spotlight, and have illuminated the silver screen and television sets.

How many black-skinned actresses have we seen on our Indian movies and TVs here? If there are a few, the directors ask their make-up staff to make these dark-skinned women fairer for the camera.

The Many Forms of Racism in India Today

We Indians are living with a strange dilemma, and we seem to use different terminologies for the same 'racism.' On one side, we oppose racism, particularly Western racism. On the other side, we don't want to recognise unexpressed internal hatred or discrimination of each other (e.g., between North Indians and South Indians) based on race. When our children are attacked either in Britain or Canada or in Australia, we shout against racial discrimination in these countries. We seem to see clearer when the subject is far away and seem less in focus when it is closer.

On one hand, we protest against racism abroad; on the other hand, we seem to patronise and support it in our own countries. When a political leader, either from the south or from Maharashtra shouts 'Why do these boys come from other states to our state and steal our jobs?' we don't find any racism there. But when a Westerner asks why are Asians stealing our jobs away, we say they are racists and we are suffering from racial discrimination. The Indians abroad feel less Indian and love to think of themselves as more Asian-Americans or Asian-Europeans than Asians or particularly South Asians. I have met some young Indians working abroad, and they feel their co-Indian colleagues (also known as 'Desi') neighbours never show any affinity towards them yet they get all types of cooperation from those Western colleagues with whom they work. It seems to be a fabrication of Bollywood movies or some popular fictions that [Indian] people abroad are always missing their motherland.

Misogyny is also a part of racism. Celia R. Daileader, a Professor of English at Florida State University (United States), and a famous feminist scholar, has identified a relationship between racism and misogyny by creating the new term

"Othello Myth" or "Othellophilia."[2] She says that Anglo-American culture's obsession with sex between black men and white women, a formula that inverts the sad realities of imperialism and slave culture, has less to do with race, *per se*, than with an imaginative appropriation of black men to control women, both black and white. She writes, "Othellophilia as a cultural construct is first and foremost about women—white women explicitly, as the 'subjects' of representation; black women implicitly, as the abjected and/or marginalised subjects of the suppressed counter-narrative (page 10)." Daileader argues that a "fear of female sexual autonomy regularly shades into fear of miscegenation (page 46)." Proving her point, Daileader asks, "Is the man who beats his daughter for sleeping with a black man (as in Jungle Fever) a sexist or a racist?"[3] She concludes, "Racism will turn to misogyny on a dime; misogyny often obscures racism."[4]

Is it a Question of Fairness?

For me, racism is bad wherever or in whatever form it takes. I am always against racism, be it in the form of attacks on Indians in Australia, or in the form of misogynic control over female sexuality through the 'Othello Myth,' or in the form of interracial feelings throughout the Indian subcontinent. What do you think?

References

1. Unesco Science Report 2005, Unesco Publishing.
2. Daileader, Celia R., *Racism, Misogyny, and the "Othello" Myth: Inter-racial Couples from Shakespeare to Spike Lee*. Cambridge University Press, 2005.
3. Ibid., p.218.
4. Ibid.

16 To be a Feminist or Not: Is it Really a Question at All?

Indian blogger Pragya Bhagat has posed a question regarding my search and conviction in her latest blogging.[1] She has admitted from the first line that her idea about a feminist is 'overexposed' with the idea that a feminist "must be aggressive. Slogan-bearing, perhaps. She must be progressive, willing to fight for what she believes in. You know, equality, education, independence, all that jazz. She doesn't have to be a 'she'."

Ms. Bhagat compared me with her nani (grandma), who was, according to her, born a decade before me, and like many elderly women, she gossips, she cooks, and criticises like none other. Although she has lived in the US for more than two decades, she is an Indian *nari* (woman) through and through. She started her own business while raising five children. She learned a new language after the age of fifty, and still works in her seventies. Pragya asked whether this description classifies her as a feminist or not. She admitted that her grandma performs 'karva chauth' (while Pragya does not), and that this fasting empowers her. According to Pragya, "at night, she dresses up in her finest jewellry and silk-embroidered sari. She performs the patient ritual of breaking the fast only when she sees the moon. Through the practice of 'karva chauth', she is celebrating herself, her self-control, and her dedication to her marriage. This is how I am beginning to perceive feminism - being the woman you are and loving it."

I am grateful to Pragya that she does a favour by comparing me with her grandma. But the total blogging, I think, is a result of a misconception, and that Pragya could not follow my ideas of feminism, though she took much pain to go through my interviews and writings. Repeatedly, I have been saying that it is odd to think that feminism is only meant to protest against male hegemony. Nowadays, feminism is a multidimensional concept, and it differs from culture to culture and from people to people.

The similarity of all the feminist ideas is the ultimate freedom of the female mass. There are different types of feminists. Some are shouting against male hegemony; some are even coming forward with their anti-sex and anti-marriage voices; some are very radical; some are very moderate; and some are sex positive. After the famous 'feminist's sex war,'[3] you can't describe fully anyone if you say 'she is a feminist.' It is also true that Pragya's study on feminism is very limited, otherwise she would not confine 'feminism' to 'slogan raising voices.'

As a creative writer, I have once mentioned that I am not an activist and that no creative writing, in my idea, should follow any 'ism.'[2] It is the philosophy which follows the writing and not what the creative writer writes that follows any 'ism.' Secondly, it's strange how Pragya could know that I keep myself away from family life or that I am different 'woman' who has no family bonding? I have to work outside; I have to manage my family; I have to cook and to take care of my household. I don't rely upon domestic help for everything. Once I was in need of a motherhood (see my story "Waiting for Manna", from my second collection of short stories), I bore and brought up my children. It is another matter that I have a husband who is very liberal and more a 'friend' to me than a 'husband' in patriarchal sense. But what makes me any day a 'feminist,' if I am ever a 'feminist' (because Pragya uttered a word 'self-described feminist' for me)? It is not due to my 'tomboy activities' in my Childhood. 'Tomboy activities' do not make anyone feminist. Rather, it is my mother, whose situation, condition, and life under the patriarchal milieu make me a 'feminist.' I have seen my father buy jewellery for her. But in India, these jewelleries are considered as an asset of a person. He (my father) did not allow my mother to wear them publicly. In my story "End of Fascination". I have pointed out that my father, along with many others of the masculine world in our society are possessive of their wives. But, they always try to discard any thought of possession over them by their wives. My story "Hatred" may be a fine example to show the reason what made me a 'feminist.'

From time to time, in my different articles, I have stated, always believed that man and woman are biologically different. I am not against any biological species. I am not against any social system like marriage, motherhood, or heterosexual love. I think man and woman are complementary to each other in order to make nature's law fulfilled. What I AM for is the same status of a female and a male in society. I am against patriarchal society but that does not mean that I want to replace a matriarchal society with a patriarchal one.

If Pragya's grandma feels fasting for her husband empowers her, I have no problem with that. My problem arises if that Grandma would force Pragya to fast during 'krava chauth' against her will, just like the patriarchal society has been doing for an eternity. Our patriarchal society has exploited sexual differences to create systems of inequality, and has exposed the facts of sexual politics. The patriarchy always tries to induce the women with three unauthentic attitudes. These are the attitude of being a 'devi' or goddess of self-less goddess (Pragya should tell me why we don't find a 'self-less' man as a god),a devoted mother, and a pure or Sati woman. These ideas are good to hear but in my opinion, they are the tools of sexual politics that patriarchy has been trying to play with women for ages. It always attempts to trap women into an impossible ideal by denying them individuality and situations for all different kinds of women. In all the three of these attitudes, women deny the original thrust of their freedom by submerging it into the object. In the case of the first, the object is herself; in the second, her beloved, and in the third, the oppression of physical and psychological needs.

Actually, to be a feminist or not to be a feminist is not at all a question. Whoever is born with a feminine gender has to remain a feminist, as her thought, sufferings, feelings, even her language and speech type are different from that of the masculine world. What is an objectionable matter to me is when someone says women are inferior or second class citizens in comparison with men.

Plato once said in his *Republic*[4] that "... the only difference between men and women is one of physical function—one begets, the other bears children. Apart from that, they both can and should perform the same functions (though men on a whole, perform them better) and should receive the same education to enable them to do so; for in this way society will get the best value from both." I admit that males can perform some functions better than women, and vice versa.

Yes it is true that some feminist thinkers and activists consider men as their main enemy. They use this idea to advertise and propagate themselves. But I think it is also similar to the idea of male hegemony. I have always tried to develop the idea that love between two people has much importance, and it should not interfere with gender equality.

I am sure, if Pragya's grandma would read my stories some day, she would applaud and find herself in my stories. Above all, we women are in the same boat, which some women like Pragya sometimes forget.

References

1. Bhagat, Pragya, "To Be or Not To Be…A Feminist", *Nazar: a South Asian Perspective*, 9 October 2009 < http://nazaronline.net/religion_culture/2009/10/to-be-or-not-to-be…a-feminist/>

2. Sarangi, Jaydeep, "In Conversation with Sarojini Sahoo." *Muse India.* Issue 28, Nov-Dec 2009. < http://www.museindia.com/showcurrent17.asp?id= 1477>
3. Ferguson, Ann, et al., "Forum: The Feminist Sexuality Debates," *Signs: Journal of Women in Culture and Society* 10(1), University of Chicago Press, 1984.
4. Bloom, Allan, Trans. *The Republic Of Plato*, Basic Books; 2 Sub edition (1991).

17 Indian Feminism and Sexual Discourse

1901

She was born into a Christian family in Bastar (now Chhatisgarh) in 1901 when her father, a doctor by profession, stayed away in Burma (now Myanmar). Later she studied medicine at Cuttack Medical School where she earned her LMP (the degree for Medical Practitioner during British Colonial times) in 1921 and started her career as the superintendent of the Cuttack Red Cross. During this time, she got involved with a fatherly person and was caught red-handed by his wife. They had physical relations, but her lover-cum-mentor wholeheartedly wished her marriage with a suitable person.

The period between 1921 and 1927 was also a productive phase of her literary life. She wrote several volumes of poems like *Anjali* and *Archana*, and novels on social issues like *Bharati* and *Parasmani* in Oriya. Through her writing, she protested against purdah, child marriage, caste system, untouchability, discrimination against women. And she advocated women's rights, steps towards their empowerment, and widow remarriage.

While working with Red Cross and also while in a relationship with her mentor lover, she got herself involved with a barefoot doctor and imposter who settled in Delhi. Her mentor was against her marriage with that unknown person, but she resigned from her service and became an Arya Samaji. She got married to that stranger and left for Delhi opened a clinic in Chandini Chowk.

She began to write in Hindi while continuing her writing in Oriya. She came out with a volume of Hindi poems entitled *Baramala.* She also became an influential editor of several Hindi periodicals such as *Mahabir*, *Jeevan* and *Nari Bharati.* Kuntala Kumari was invited to deliver the convocation addresses at Allahabad University and at Benaras Hindu University. That was a mark of rare recognition accorded to a woman of those days.

But her marital life was not happy, and her husband exploited her as a source of income against which she wanted to resist. She died at only 37 years of age with illness and mental trauma. Eminent Hindi novelist Jainendra Kumar's novel *Kalyani* was based on her struggle and her pathetic life.

She was Kuntala Kumari Sabat[1] the veteran feminist poetess and writer of Oriya Literature. Though her pre- and post-marital life were not so peaceful and her life was dangling between love, sex, oppression, and harassment by the male-dominated mentality of feudal India, we never find any sexual agony or any of her own saga of life in her poems. Rather she always tried to hide her sexual expression with a coated version of mysticism in the form of Sufi ideology. This trend prevailed for many years, and even after few decades in the beginning of the post-colonial era we see that the poetess expressed her feelings of love in the form of Bhakti poems.

1914

In 1930, a Romanian young boy met a 16-year-old Indian girl and they fell in love. The boy had come to India to study Indian philosophy and the girl was his teacher's daughter. They couldn't hide this affair and were soon caught by the mentor. The boy was asked to leave the mentor's residence and, never to contact the girl again.

Later, the boy became a world, famous philosopher and wrote a semi-autobiographical novel first published in Romania in 1933. It was written specifically for a literary prize and sold very well in Romania, garnering both fame and money. The novel was translated into Italian in 1945, into German in 1948, into French in 1950, and into Spanish in 1952.

The girl was married at the age of twenty and had two children. She engaged herself in writing and published volumes of poetry and prose, wrote many books on Tagore, but was not famous until 1974.

However, the girl was not aware of that Romanian novel until she heard about it from her father who had visited Europe in 1938 or 1939. She also came to know that the book was also dedicated to her. But it was not until 1972, when a close Romanian friend of the author came to Kolkata, and she finally understood that the author had described a sexual relationship between them in his book. She subsequently had a friend who translated the novel for her from the French; she was shaken by his depictions. In 1973, when she went to America to attend a seminar on Tagore, she met the author again after 43 years and talked personally to him. She also warned him that she would sue him if his book ever came out in English. The author assured her that he wouldn't publish the English version of his novel. But perhaps she didn't believe the author and she herself couldn't check her agony—the agony of her love being misrepresented. So she wrote a novel.

Later, after her death in 1974, the University of Chicago Press published the English translation of both the Romanian and Indian novels, both as companion volumes depicting two sides of a romance. In her novel, she wanted to paint how an Indian girl fell in love with a Western boy, depicting the whole thing as being more concerned with emotion rather than with physical co-adherence.

The Romanian author was Mircea Eliade and the Indian girl was Maitreyi Devi. The English translation of the Romanian novel is entitled *The Bengal Nights*[2] while the English translation of the Indian novel is entitled *It Does Not Die.*[3]

1919

After six years of dating incidents of Maiytreyi, a young poetess of Punjab married an editor of a literary magazine. She was engaged to him in early childhood and changed her name. Later she became the author of 70 works, which included novels, short stories and poems. She was elected a fellow of the Sahitya Akademi, in India, as one of the 21 immortals of literature. She was honoured with the Padma Vibhushan, the Jnanpith Award and the Padma Shree. She also received three D Lit degrees from Delhi, Jabalpur, and Vishva Bharti Universities.

She was born in 1919 in Gujranwala, now in Pakistan, the only child of a school teacher, a poet and an editor of a literary journal. When she was 40 years old, she got herself involved with an Urdu poet and left her husband, but that Urdu poet did not prepare to marry her as he had a new woman in his life. Later, she became involved with another painter and lived the last 40 years of her life with that artist, who also designed most of her book covers. For the rest of her life, she maintained her two lovers with equal potency of love and without any confrontation.[4]

The author was Amrita Pritam, who died on October 31, 2005, and her two lovers were Imroz and Sahir Ludhianvi. Penguin India has published a book entitled *Amrita-Imroz: A Love Story* by Uma Trilok.

1934

In 1934, after four years of romance of Maitreyi-Eliade, a Keralite girl was born and spent her childhood in that city. She began writing at the age of 17 in both Malayalam and English.

At the age of 15, she got married to a man 15 years older than her, and their first son was born after only one year of their marriage.

In her writing, she soon got involved in controversies as her writings were a type of confession where she did not hide her sufferings and her traumas that started from her teenage years and then went on and on. She was the first woman writer to write and discuss about her sexual desires in her writings. She did not hide in her writings either her lesbian relationships or her husband's homosexual tendencies, nor did she hide her extra-marital relationships. But strangely enough, her husband always supported her writings.

In Chapter 27 of her most discussed and controversial autobiographical book *My Story,* she writes, "During my nervous breakdown, there developed between myself and my husband an intimacy which was purely physical ... after bathing me in warm water and dressing me in men's clothes, my husband bade me sit on his lap, fondling me and calling me his little darling boy.... I was by nature shy... but during my illness, I shed my shyness and for the first time in my life learned to surrender totally in bed with my pride intact and blazing."[5]

Though in numerous interviews, she praised her husband for showing his support for her writings, in her book *My Story*, she told that her husband supported her writings because her writings were a source of income for him. However, he died after a long illness. She later tried her luck at politics and failed.

At the age of 65, she converted herself become Muslim to marry a young man. After converting herself thus, she argued that purdah in Islam was the most wonderful dress for women in the world. And she had always loved to wear the purdah as it gives women a sense of security. Only Islam gives protection to women. About her conversion to Islam, she told that she had been lonely all through her life. At night, she used to sleep by embracing a pillow. But she was no longer a loner.

Islam was her company. According to her, Islam is the only religion in the world that gives love and protection to women. But in 2006, she issued a statement at a book release ceremony organised by Kairali Books in Kochi that she deeply regretted converting to Islam and was disillusioned with the treacherous behaviour of her Muslim friends. She claimed that all her wealth amounting to several lakhs, gold ornaments, books and other valuables had been looted by them.

She was Kamala Das or Madhavikutty or Kamala Surraiyah. She had been shortlisted for the Nobel Prize for literature in 1984 along with Marguerite Yourcenar, Doris Lessing and Nadine Gordimer. Apart from that, she received many awards for her literary contributions, like the Asian Poetry Prize, Kent Award for English Writing from Asian Countries, Asian World Prize, Sahitya Academy Award Kerala Sahitya Academy Award, etc. She passed away on 31 May 2009 in Pune at the age of 75.

The Role of Sexuality from a Colonial Perspective

These four feminist writers of the last century tried to raise their voices, which apparently may seem very contradictory, confusing and even delineating different values for feminine aspects. Following the work of these feminists, anyone can argue that womanhood is, as a whole, a paradigmatic myth, which incorporates multiple myths of the woman in a mystic form. We have no way to oppose this parenthesis. But as a female (please note that I am not saying the word 'feminist'), I can feel every situation was true for me if any day I would be either Maitreyi or Kamala or Amrita or Kuntala. It is a very vague argument why Maitreyi was not like Kamala or Amrita was not like Kuntala. Maitreyi could admit her relationship with Eliade as Kamala did. Why didn't Amrita bear all her pathos as Kuntala did? These are vague arguments.

I think the transformation of a woman's heart from Kuntala to Kamala must be possible due to the development of feminism in India. The reason and development of feminism in India is different from that of the Western world. The pre-colonial social structure and the role of women revealed in them was theorised into feminism. It was more a social than any individual matter. Female mass was considered equal to male mass but the status of the individual female body remained as puritan as it was in feudalistic patriarchal society. In pre-colonial India, we see that plural marriage was allowed for males and even we find our male intellectuals, writers, politicians were able to get married to another woman in the case of the death of their first wife. It is also ironically true that the female mortality rate was considerably higher in comparison with males due to lack of proper nutrition. But we never find a single instance of any woman remarrying after becoming a widow in those days, though the marriage of widows was legalised from the early days of British rule.

Women were taught to act as a goddess of sacrifice, and as Simone tells us in her *The Second Sex*[6], the women were trapped into an impossible ideal (the myth of the mother, the virgin, the motherland, nature, etc.) by denying individuality to women. So when our pre-colonial feminists used to write essays, they often chose titles like "Women's Duty for Household" or "The Legendary Female Figures in Indian Myths," where the patriarchal tone was still there. So an attempt to reconstruct Indian womanhood as the essence of Indian culture through the nationalist movement can be seen where the individual feminism was deliberately denied. Kuntala and Maitreyi were products of these pre-colonial societies.

The largest and the leading women's organisation in India at this time was the All-India Women's Conference. A wing of the Indian National Congress, it was founded in 1927, was many-layered, and always attempted to reflect the regional diversity of the movement. Within one year of Maitreyi-Elliad's meeting at Kolkata, the Indian National Congress passed the Karachi Resolution in 1931 where 'swaraj' or 'self-rule' in free India was declared, but the gender issue was still marginalised as evidenced by the fact that only one of the resolutions expressly mentions protecting women's rights (as part of workers' rights).

Undoubtedly, post-colonial India was different from that of pre-colonial India, and women's education was flourishing. And the age-old binaries that had characterised dominant philosophical and political thinking on gender were reconstructed with an array of oppressive patriarchal family structures: age, ordinal status, relationship to men through family of origin, marriage, and procreation, as well as patriarchal attributes: dowry, siring sons, etc., kinship, caste, community, village, market, and the state were put into questionable range. Along with these questions, 'rights of women's bodies' are also seen as antithetical to these patriarchal milieus.

I have to write this article in support of Kamala Das or Amrita Pritam because some of our scholars always try to carve a separate identity for sexuality other than feminism. They define feminism in order to avoid uncritical following as the protest for male hegemony and in their conception, sexuality has no role to protest against such hegemony. If feminist writing during the twentieth century colonial India was characterised by societal hierarchies, and a need to demarcate an Indian identity, feminist debates in post-colonial India dealt with ways in which feminist sexualities were practised. This is why the whole country mourns the demise of Amrita and Kamala

References

1. Ray, Pratibha, *Kuntala Kumari Sabat (Oriya Poet)*, Delhi: Sahitya Akademy.
2. Eliade, Mircea, *Bengal Nights*, Trans. Catherine Spencer, University Of Chicago Press, 1995.

3. Devi, Maitreyi, *It Does Not Die*, Trans. Maitreyi Devi, University Of Chicago Press.
4. Pritam, Amrita, *The Revenue Stamp: An Autobiography*, Trans. Krishna Gorowara, Stosius Inc/Advent Books Division, 1983.
5. Das, Kamala, *My Story*, Harper Collins India, (Special Edition: 2009).
6. Beauvoire, Simone, Trans. H. M. Parshley, *The Second Sex*, Penguin (reprint edition, 1972).

18 Lonely in the Crowd

The Bhakti movement in Indian literature focused on singular devotion, mystical love for God, and had a particular focus on a personal relationship with the Divine. Given their belief in the centrality of personal devotion, poet-saints were highly critical of ritual observances as maintained and fostered by the Brahmin priesthood. Though the Bhakti movement had its genesis in southern India in the sixth century AD, it didn't gain momentum until the twelfth century in the central western regions of India. It then moved northward, coming to an end roughly in the seventeenth century.

But strangely enough, if we compare the gender basis participation ratio of saint-poets, we find the inclusion of women in this movement was tempered. It is also true that there is little evidence to support any type of revolt against the patriarchal norms of the time. Women *bhaktas* (disciples) were simply staying largely within the patriarchal ideology that upheld the chaste and dutiful wife as ideal. These women transferred the object of their devotion and their duties as the "lovers" or "wives" to their divine lover or husband. None the less, that their poetry became an integral aspect of the Bhakti movement at large is highly significant and inspirational for many who look to these extraordinary women as ideal examples of lives intoxicated by love for the Divine.

Andal Thiruppavai (a tenth century Tamil poetess), Akka Mahadevi (a twelfth century Kannad poetess), Janabai (a thirteenth century Marathi poetess), Meera Bai of sixteenth century in Hindi and Madhavi Dasi in that century in Oriya literature were some poetesses who wrote exquisite poetry which have been passed on through bards and singers throughout India. But strangely enough, they had to face challenges from the patriarchal society, whereas no male poets of their time had to encounter such bitter experiences. These female poets were often blamed by their husbands for going against marital practices while there was no evidence that the wives of the male poet-saints raised voices against the divine love affairs of their husbands.

Akka Mahadevi as well as Meera accepted her God as her husband. There were some poet-saints who were devotees of the Goddess 'Shakti; or Kali, but for these saints, the Goddess appeared to them as a mother rather than a wife. The 'Kali-Sadhaka-Poets' of Eastern India always painted Goddess Kali as their mother but not as their wives.

But Sri Chaitanya Dev, in fifteenth century, started a 'Raganuga bhakti marga' in which the God—Krishna—remained male, and the disciples loved him with a 'sakhi bhava.' In Sanskrit, 'sakhi' means 'girlfriend.' As most of the disciples of Sri Chaitanya Dev were males, the male disciples had to assume themselves as 'female' ones and as 'sweethearts of God; strangly enough to mark that this identity, crossing and trouping of the sexual self-did not touch gendering. And out of 191 devotees listed in the *Chaitanya Charitamrita*[1], a biographical reference book of Chaitanya cult, only 17 were women; five of them were members of Chaitanya's direct family.

Abhimanyu Samanta Singhar, a remarkable Oriya poet and follower of Sri Chaitanya, wrote in his poems, "Whenever Goddess Radha calls me, I will respond to her call as a sincere maid." But they had patriarchal misogynist values in spite of the exalted place that it gives to a female deity, Radha, and to the feminine virtues, and in spite of the fact that these disciples were highly inclined towards the feminine soul lying within them to feel themselves as "Radha', the lover of Lord Krishna.

The *Chaitanya Charitamrita*, the great holy book of the Chaitanya cult, which stresses on the universality of devotion and denies any disqualifications based on birth, sex or caste, seemed not to have had any influence on the status of women. The book depicts a strong belief that the role of women continues to be a supporting one and subordinate to that of men. In the case of sexuality, though it denied any active association of a feminine world, it created a cultural setback in sixteenth century Orissa, as this state was the centre for such movements with royal support. Vaishnavism started mundane sex among the disciples of Sri Chaitanya Dev in the form of both heterosexuality and homosexuality.

Madhavi Dasi was one of few women disciples of Sri Chaitanyya Dev, and she remained in direct contact with the saint. She was an Oriya poet who used to write her poems both in Oriya and Braja-boli. The author Haridas Das has mentioned in his book *Gaudiya Vaishnava Abhidhana*[2] that Madhavi Dasi composed a Sanskrit play about Lord Jagannath, *PuruSottama-deva-Natakam*. If this is true, she is a single exception as the first female playwright of India and also the only female author of a Sanskrit text in the Bhakti movement tradition. Madhavi Dasi was the sister of Sikhi Mohanty, a close associate of Sri Chaitanya Dev, and was a member of Chaitanya's most exclusive inner circle. According to *Chaitanya Charitamrita*, as described by Krishna Das Kaviraj, Madhavi was in love with another disciple by the name of Junior Haridas, and they both were punished by Sri Chaitanya Dev for their activities.

Though the Chaitanya cult possessed misogynist ideas, the life of Chaitanya was far from misogynic. Sri Chaitanya was twice married and had a good relationship with the wives of his disciples. These females were devotees of Sri Chaitanya rather than Krishna, and their high status in the hierarchy of

Chaitanya's associates is due primarily to the relation which they had to him. They are considered to be eternal associates who descended with him to participate in his 'lila', the so-called divine play by the mentor.

Chaitanya Charitamrita, the biography of the Vaishnavite saint, describes how the Mahaprabhu (as the saint was called by his disciples) overwhelmed emotionally upon hearing verses from the *Gita Govinda*[3] being sung by a woman. He rushed to embrace the singer, oblivious to her sex. Only when he was tackled by his servant Govinda Das did he come to his senses and realised the magnitude of what he had been about to do.

I am sure that if Madhavi Dasi had had any relationship with Sri Chaitanya, then the tone of *Chaitanya Charitamrita* would have changed. Despite being described as an infidel woman, Madhavi has been described as a glorious holy woman.

Religious morality often becomes a patriarchal misogyny, where society wants to see a woman as a passive sex receptacle rather than an equal sex partner, and always demands that she should not use her body for her own pleasure, instead preserve it for her husband, mentor or master. There's a reason they use the word 'purity' to describe women's virginity. What about the mentor or social guru, when he doesn't control his own sexuality? Often, his activities are glamourised with a divine description rather than being condemned as done to a woman.

I think misogyny is a critical part of sexism and is always used with religion, culture and ethics, having a double standard, where the same rules have never been applied for masculine subjects.

Madhavi Dasi was a victim of patriarchal Vaishnavism. She was a victim of Sri Chaitanya Dev's misogyny. She was also a victim of her time. But very few lines have been written in support of her after hundreds of years of those events. And no feminist critic has come in support of that great writer except the one-line citation about Madhavi Dasi in Gayatri Chakravorty Spivak's essay *Moving Devi*.[4]

In this article I want to attribute my support for the struggle Madhavi Dasi had to face a few centuries ago to prove her right over her own body. She was truly...lonely in the crowd.

Notes and References

1. *Chaitanya Charitamruta* is one of the primary biographies detailing the life and teachings of Chaitanya Mahaprabhu (1486-1533), a Vaishnava saint, written by Krishnadasa Kaviraja Goswami.
2. Das, Haridas, *Goudiya Vaishnaba Abidhan*, Nabadwip, West Bengal: Haribol Kutir, 1964.
3. The *Gita Govinda* is the best known composition of Jayadeva, who lived in Orissa, AD circa 1200. The first English translation of the *Gita Govinda* was published by Sir William Jones in 1792. Since then, the *Gita Govinda* has been translated into many languages throughout the world, and is considered to be among the finest examples of Sanskrit poetry.
4. Spivak, Gayatri Chakravorty, "Moving Devi", *Other Asias*, Wiley-Blackwell, 2007.

19 The Ambiguities of Feminine Identity

A love affair between two poets belonging to two different languages in the early twentieth century in India is very little known. I even found many Bengali readers and writers unaware of this fact. The true love story was discovered by Oriya poet Kabibara Radhanath Roy and Bengali poetess Nagendra Bala Ray.

This depicts the sexual politics of the nineteenth century's patriarchal milieu.

Kabibar Radhanath Ray, the prime figure of Oriya literature, who freed poetry from medieval clasp and with the influence of Romantic English poets like Wordsworth, Coleridge and Keats, designed Oriya poetry by introducing new forms, new topics, a new approach and greater freedom. Among the many new things which he brought into Oriya poetry, there were blank-verse, pictorial, musical but direct and unambiguous language following Scott and Wordsworth, satire in the manner of Dryden and Pope, denunciation of despots, tyrants and oppressors, concern with social problems, a spirit of protest against conventional morality, a disbelief in the power of gods and goddesses, and patriotic sentiments, which last brought him trouble from his employers. He was viewed as a national poet of the first order in Orissa.

Radhanath was born on 28 September 1848, at Kedarpur village in Balasore district, and in his early life, he composed in both Bengali and Oriya languages but later shifted his writings to Oriya only. He started his carrier as a teacher in Balasore Zilla School and later was promoted to Inspector of Schools. In January 1900, he was transferred to Burdwan, a semi-urban town of Bengal, where there he met Nagendra Bala.

Nagendra Bala was married to a Sub-Registrar of Jamalpur, and besides her two poetry books *Marma Gatha* and *Prem Gatha*, she authored a prose book on taboos for females, where she wrote about the do's and don'ts for the fairer sex. When she met Radhanath, he was 53 and she was 25; they fell in love. Bala was so impressed by Radhanath's poetry that she learnt Oriya to read his poems in their original form. *Dhabaleswar*, one of her poetry books, was even dedicated to 'motherly Ms.Parashmani Devi, the wife of veteran Oriya poet Radhanath Roy.'

Nagendra Bala became impressed with one of Radhanath's poems, which was written much before her birth and in which he wrote: "I want to bow my head to the feet of Nagendra Bala." Actually the word 'Nagendra Bala' is a synonym for 'mountain,' but it impressed Nagendra Bala, the poet, and she romantically began to think that Radhanath had been waiting for her since before her birth.

Bala died at the age of 28 in 1906. After her death, Radhanath suffered mental trauma, and he wanted to confess his sin for involving himself with his extramarital affairs. He wrote a confessional letter, printed it, and circulated it among all the editors, writers, poets, and readers of Oriya and Bengali literature with a request to make the copies of this mail and to forward it to as many people as possible.

In his personal social prejudices, Radhanath was as misogynistic as any man of his time, and held traditional, stereotypical and patriarchal views of women, which he sometimes explicitly committed to writing in letters and notebooks. But his writings often portrayed female characters in his long poems (in Oriya they are called 'Kavyas') as pro-female. During his time he was criticised by the critics for dealing with sexuality in his poems such as in *Jajati,Nandikeswari* and *Parvati.*

These contradictions were prevailing in society of that time and we find many of our writers and intellectuals of that time had more than one wife during their lifespan. But it was hoped that after the death of a husband, a female would maintain her life without marrying others.

There was another very reputed personality in Orissa, the esteemed Gopal Chandra Praharaj. He authored the first and largest ever Oriya dictionary-cum-linguistic encyclopedia which was a magnum opus. Keeping his wife in a remote village, he used to live with his sister-in-law Pitambari Devi at his residence in Cuttack. He was in love with her but to prove himself socially monogamous, he did not marry her. When one day he found out that his wife was involved in a love affair with one of their servants in the village, he rushed there. He called his son and wife and confronted them asking for social justice. When I read these events from the biography of Pitambari Devi, I couldn't help but shiver at the thought that these social milieus in my beloved country had passed its glorious days.

I have no less respect for these two authors now. In fact, I bow my head to them and feel intensely grateful to them because if they had not been there, I would not have found my language and literature in as such a prestigious spot as it currently is in the Indian subcontinent.

What irritates me, though, is the social system of that time. Either consciously or unconsciously, that social system had oppressed women, allowing them little or no voice in the political, social or economic issues of that time. And now I think we are miles away from these milieus, and I am thankful for my predecessor feminists who fought their best to change the destiny of women.

I don't find anything wrong with Nagendra Bala and with the legal wife of G.C.Praharaj. Rather, I consider their male partners as pseudo and virtual. In my country, I have noted that the eminent personalities here have a tendency to create a self-image of sainthood to the public as the masses also search for sainthood among public figures. This is the main difference between India and the West.

Here, Italian Sonia Gandhi has to cover her head to prove that she has turned herself into the typical ideal Indian woman, whereas in America, nobody cares about the sexy dresses of Michelle Obama. It doesn't mean that the American society is totally getting rid of patriarchal attitudes. In some ways, in fact, the United States is more patriarchal than puritanical. But in India, the attitude of the males for a state of sexual promiscuity in a particular order remains for the moment, while opposing that status for the females which remains without a satisfactory answer.

Once the writer George Elliot (1819-1880) wrote in her novel *Felix Holt*[4] that a woman can hardly ever choose; she is dependent on what happens to her. She must take meaner things, because only meaner things are within her reach. George Elliot was somehow a contemporary to Radhanath but lived in the other part of the globe. But her assumption on female destiny was not more different from that of Indian women of the time. When we think about the destiny of Nagendra Bala or Praharaj's wife, a question may arise: Why have these complaints appeared just two or three centuries ago? And why don't more echoes of the feminine revolt and oppressive situation exist?

In both parts of the globe, women were criticised and repudiated for their sexuality by a male-dominated society. The social gurus always have treated the question of women's liberation and sexual freedom only from the negative point of view. They have never tried to compare the question with the status of the male. Sex-positive women were not simply misinformed, or priggish or neurotic. Rather, they were often rationally responding to their material reality. Their orgasm was denied and only two choices had been left for them: (1) passive and usually pleasure-less submission, with the high risk of undesirable consequences or (2) rebellious refusal.

This is what happened with Nagendra Bala and Mrs. Praharaj. After his confession regarding his 'sinful affair' with a married lady, the image of Radhanath was enhanced in the society of that time. He was regarded as a 'saint of saints' for the courage to confess his sins. Nagendra Bala, on the other hand, was painted as a sexist woman who was responsible for the said affair, and some critics have also stated that the evil intention of that lady may have been to trap a 'saintly' personality.

One point to note is that nobody has ever asked how Nagendra Bala was crossed if Radhanath had no willingness to cross her.

I am interested in searching for other aspects of the affair with a view to male sexual politics, and in particular, to discover if there is another tradition running alongside moral conservation and social purity in which men tried to assert the possibilities of a different kind of sexual life for them; one that didn't involve their systematic subordination.

If there is such an aspect of our history, a collective effort on the part of women worldwide, to develop a language and politics of sexual pleasure as well as sexual protection, is greatly needed to conform with our feminist thoughts.

Reference

1. Eliot, George, *Felix Holt, the Radical*, Ed. Lynda Mugglestone, Penguin Classics, 1995.

20 Beyond Misogyny

It is ironic that in India, the premier persons who came forward to claim 'women's rights' were not women but were men. Balaram Das, a sixteenth century poet, very well known inside Orissa but lesser known to the outside world, is considered as an exponent of feminism. As feminism developed in Western countries around the seventeenth century, it is to be noted that Balaram Das pointed out the male hegemony of patriarchal society in his poems much before it began in the Europe.

In 1617, John Swetnam's misogynist pamphlet "The Arraignment of Women" (1615) induced English women to enter the debate on the woman question that had been boiling on the continent for two centuries. Rachel Speght, who was the first English woman to protest against Mr. Swetnam with almost the same line of argument, directly claimed that women are not inferior to men in intellectual ability.

In 1673, François Poulain de La Barre, a disciple of Descartes, published a book entitled *Essays Concerning the Equality of Men and Women*, where he straightforwardly pointed out that women are, by nature, no less intelligent than men, and that they would be able to engage in both creative and intellectual vocations if they were provided with the opportunity to study at educational institutions as men were. He further insists that the view of females as socially and intellectually defective is derived from the blind acceptance of the comments of various classical philosophers about women.

It is not a mere coincidence that strong defences of women's abilities appeared in two different countries in the seventeenth century. Sandra Gilbert and Susan Gubar, in their book *The Madwoman in the Attic*[1] tended to examine Victorian literature from a feminist perspective; they also quote and admit the role of Milton's *Paradise Lost* in these feminist terminologies.

John Milton (born in 1608) was an English poet, best known for his epic *Paradise Lost.* He was writing at a time of religious and political instability in England. His poetry and prose reflected deep convictions, often reacting to contemporary circumstances; but it is not always easy to locate the writer in an obvious religious category, although his views may be described as broadly Protestant. He was an accomplished, scholarly man of letters, a polemical writer, and an official in the government of Oliver Cromwell.

On the other hand, the reputed medieval saint poet of sixteenth century, Balaram Das, one of the five poet companions revivalists of Vaishnavism, popularly known as *Panchasakha*, has a significant effect on Oriya literature. His *Lakshmi Purana* provided the other pillar on which subsequent literature was to thrive, and was considered as the first manifesto of Women's Liberation and Feminism in Indian Literature. But it was written to promote a Hindu ritual 'Vrat/ Brat.' (*Vrat* or Brat are the Hindu rituals of fasting or Upavas, mainly observed by the women, to please a particular God or Goddesses on a particular day. when devotees refrain themselves from food or water.Every Vrat/Brat has its own 'puranas' or legend describe in mythical poem form, which were to be recited at the rituals).

The tragedy of Adam and Eve is the central theme of *Paradise Lost.* It contains two arcs: one of Satan (Lucifer) and another of Adam and Eve. The story of Satan continues the epic convention of large-scale warfare. It begins after Satan and the other rebel angels have been defeated and cast down by God into Hell.

The story of Adam and Eve's temptation and fall is a fundamentally different, new kind of epic: a domestic one. Adam and Eve are presented for the first time in Christian literature as having a functional relationship while still without sin. They have passions, personalities and sex. Satan successfully tempts Eve by preying on her vanity and tricking her with rhetoric, and Adam, seeing Eve has sinned, knowingly commits the same sin by also eating of the fruit. In this manner, Milton portrays Adam as a heroic figure but also as a deeper sinner than Eve. After eating the fruit, they have lustful sex. Both experience new and negative emotions, particularly the powerful pair of guilt and shame, and engage in mutual recrimination. However, Eve's pleas to Adam reconcile them somewhat. More importantly, her encouragement enables them both to approach God, to "bow and sue for grace with suppliant knee," to receive grace from God. Adam goes on a vision journey with an angel where he witnesses the errors of man and the Great Flood, and he is saddened by the sin that they have released through the consumption of the fruit. However, he is also shown hope—the possibility of redemption–through a vision of Jesus Christ. They are then cast out of Eden and the archangel Michael says that Adam may find "A paradise within thee, happier far." They now have a more distant relationship with God, who is omnipresent but invisible (unlike the previous tangible Father in the Garden of Eden).

Lakshmi Purana is also a popular poem in Orissa and it has a great religious ritualistic value as the female masses of Orissa celebrate a 'brata'. Every Thursday in the Margashira month of the Hindu calendar, they recite the poem as a ritual during their worship to Lakshmi, the goddess of wealth. *The Lakshmi Purana* is also translated into English, in prosaic form, by Dr. Jagannath Prasad Das.[2]

In Balaram Das's *Lakshmi Purana*, critics find a typical patriarchal dilemma, and though he was a supporter of feminism, he couldn't ideologically place himself above the patriarchal moral values about the female masses. In the beginning of the *Lakshmi Purana*, he describes the "do's and don'ts" of a woman. "Many things are taboo for women during this period: giving Mahalakshmi's Prasad to outsiders, even to the married daughter; beating the children; not cleaning the cooking vessels till all the black is gone; spreading the bed crooked; disobeying the in-laws; sleeping naked; applying oils; and so on. If it happens to be the last day of the dark fortnight on Thursday, a woman should not wash the mouth after meals; face south or west while eating; tie and dress hair in the evening; eat in a dark room; apply oil on the body after bath; be angry with or disobey the husband. Lakshmi does not leave the house of the woman who treats her husband as god, is of clean habits, and shares her husband's happiness and sorrow. She shuns the house of the woman who is adulterous, lazy, dirty, quarrelsome and disrespectful to the husband. The married woman has no future without her husband. If she does so leaving aside service to her husband, she is destined to be reborn as a child widow."[3]

But the later part of *Lakshmi Purana* reveals another story. The so-called 'devoted wife' moral value supporter Goddess Lakshmi had to face a setback from her husband Lord Jagannath and her husband's elder brother Lord Balaram. Seeing her as a member of a low caste from Chandal's house, the elder brother of Lord Jagannath became enraged and asked his brother, Lord Jagannath, to 'drive her out.' According to Lord Balaram, "A wife is like a pair of sandals. If you have your brother, you can have ten million wives. If you still feel for your wife, go and build a palace in the Chandala Street (the street where untouchables reside: my addition to the text); don't come back to my great temple."[4]

Lakshmi said, "You want to throw me out since I stayed a while in the house of an untouchable. You talk of caste and since you are gods, everything is excused. What about your own caste? You lived in a cowherd's house. You ate in Nima's house; you ate leftover fruits from Jara. Both you brothers are therefore low caste, no less. If the wife makes a mistake, the husband must bear it. For one transgression, the master does not remove his servant."[5]

The following text describes how Lakshmi, being driven away from her in-law's house, established herself by making a palace; the Goddess then summoned the eight Vetalas and asked them to ransack the kitchen and pantry in the temple, and bring everything to her. The story later tells how the two gods lord Jagannath and Lord Balaram, decided to go out begging. Wearing torn clothes, a sacred thread on the shoulder and a broken umbrella in hand, the brothers now looking like Brahmin beggars, went round asking for water to drink. Lakshmi then called Saraswati, and asked her to go to every house and ask the householders not to give food and water to Jagannath. So wherever the two gods went, they were taken to be thieves and driven out. At last, the two brothers had to surrender to Goddess Lakshmi, and agreed that she could live wherever she wanted and the two gods would never again try to forbid her.

Balaram Das never tried to raise his tone directly on the moral values of patriarchal society. But very tactfully, he raised his voice against the Hindu patriarchal system. Similarly, Milton had never raised his voice against Christianity but he raised his voice in support of sexuality. Balaram Das skipped the topic of sexuality but placed himself, instead, as a supporter of feminism within the limitations of a marriage.

The relationship between Adam and Eve in *Paradise Lost* is one of "...mutual dependence, not a relation of domination or hierarchy." Hermine Van Nuis clarifies that although there is a sense of stringency associated with the specified roles of the male and the female, each unreservedly accepts the designated role because it is viewed as an asset.[6]

But in *Lakshmi Purana*, we find that the husband Lord Jagannath is more inclined to the patriarchal values, and his relationship with Lakshmi overstates the independence of the characters' stances and therefore, misses the way in which Adam and Eve are entwined with each other." On the other hand, Goddess Lakshmi asserts her independence while recalling her marriage days, while questioning the gods about their view of the caste system and when wanting to live separately from her husband, Lord Jagannath. Attitudes in the *Purana* show Lakshmi to be of a strong personality to protest chauvinistic and incorrect male perspectives. Thus a positive outlook in her character on feminist ideology can be witnessed in the *Laksmi Purana.* But in comparison to Laksmi, Eve was a weak character. Though in the beginning, Eve displays her independence while gazing into a pool and seeing her own image.

Though Milton appeared as a pro-feminist in his free verse epic *Paradise Lost,* critics blame him for his misogynist attitude[7] whereas there was no evidence of misogynism in Balaram Das. The sexual right is the main topic for Eve in *Paradise Lost.* Though Balaram Das wants to skip the sexual topics, still both the poets have made their stand nearer to the social right and social freedom of the feminine masses. It is also an amazing fact to mark that the pro-feminist voice was raised in the Eastern world at least hundred years before the Western world could think over it.

References

1. Gilbert, Sandra and Gubar, Susan, *The Madwoman in the Attic,* Yale University Press, 2000.
2. Das, Jagannath Prasad, "English Version of *Lakshmi purana*", *Manushi,* No.73, November-December 1992.
3. Ibid.
4. Ibid.
5. Ibid.
6. Van Nuis, H. (May 2000), "Animated Eve Confronting Her Animus: A Jungian Approach to the Division of Labor Debate in Paradise Lost", *Milton Quarterly* 34 (2): pp. 48-56
7. Gallagher, Philip J., *Milton, the Bible, and Misogyny,* Univ of Missouri Pr, 1990.

21 Yes, They are Others

Plato once said in his *Republic* that "the only difference between men and women is one of physical function—one begets, the other bears children. Apart from that, they both can and should perform the same functions (though men on a whole perform them better) and should receive the same education to enable them to do so; for in this way society will get the best value from both."

Our society has grown into a polar dichotomy system of male and female, where the former oppresses the latter and treats them as the 'other' or similar to the lower caste.

Patriarchy is just one of the hierarchies, where females are the most oppressed in the traditional system. Feminist argument for sexual equality works in two directions. First, it exposes the ways in which patriarchy exploits the sexual difference to create systems of inequality, and exposes the facts of sexual politics, which later leads to feminism to fight against male hegemony. It also claimed that so long as the standard of equality is the male body, the discriminatory sexual difference remains in play. Second, it acts as a prime source for the 'others' theory developed by Simone de Beauvoire in a later period.

Simone adopted the idea of 'others' from Hegelian theory. The German philosopher Hegel was among the first to introduce the idea of the 'other' as a constituent in self-consciousness. He wrote of pre-self-conscious Man: "Each consciousness pursues the death of the other", meaning that in seeing separateness between one and another, a feeling of alienation is created, which one tries to resolve by synthesis. The resolution is depicted in Hegel's famous parable of the master slave dialectic.[1] While laying stress to explain woman's definition as man's 'other' or her consequent oppression, at the same time Simone tackles the way in which the preceding analyses (biological, historical, psychoanalytic, etc.) contribute to the formulation of the myth of the "Eternal Feminine".[2] This paradigmatic myth, which incorporates multiple myths of woman under it (such as the myth of the mother, the virgin, the motherland, nature, etc.), attempts to trap woman into an impossible ideal by denying the individuality and situation of all different kinds of women. In fact, the ideal set by the Eternal Feminine sets up an impossible expectation because the various manifestations of the myth of femininity appear as contradictory and doubled. But it is also true that for their "Eternal Feminine" women are forced to relinquish their claims to transcendence and authentic subjectivity by a progressively more stringent acceptance of the "passive" and "alienated" role.

I fully agree with Simone when she says that women can free themselves by "thinking, taking action, working, creating, on the same terms as men; instead of seeking to disparage them, she declares herself their equal." But my point is that though women need the same status as man in being seen as a human being, I think they have their own identity and they are different from men. They are 'others' in real definition but this is not in context with the Hegelian definition of "others". It is not always due to man's "active" and "subjective" demands.

Simone herself also denies her statement in the discussion of *The Ethics of Ambiguity*. She discusses three particular inauthentic attitudes in which women hide their freedom in: "The Narcissist," "The Woman in Love," and "The Mystic."

In all these three, women deny the original thrust of their freedom by submerging it into the object; in the case of the first, the object is herself; in the second, her beloved; and in the third, the Absolute or God. I don't believe its only masculine activities, but some biological facts are also responsible for the slavery. But it is true that some of the social structures made the woman as "others", if we consider these "others" as slaves (as Hegel used the word to describe the actual position of slaves).

References

1. Taylor,Charles, *Hegel and Modern Society*, New York: Cambridge University Press, 1979.
2. Beauvoir, Simone de, *The Second Sex, 1949*, Trans. H. M. Parshley, Penguin, 1972.

22 Pleasure on Par

There is a misconception among Indian feminists that in ancient days, women were observing their fundamental rights, including the right over their own body and mind. Mythical characters like Kunti, Madri, Mandodari, Draupadi are often referred to for their polygamist activities. But had they truly adopted polygamy for their own will ? Vyasa's *Mahabharata* tells us about the strange traditions of 'niyoga' in which a woman was allowed to have sexual activities for bearing of offspring. This custom was allowed because in Hindu beliefs a son is necessary for a man. He cannot go to heaven unless he has progeny. That is why Ambika and Ambalika were forced to have intercourse with their brother-in-law Vyasa. Pandu, the husband of Kunti, was a strange psychic person. He was impotent and his sexual frustration made him marry two wives, Kunti and Madri, and perhaps this sexual frustration revealed by the story of Pandu later killing the two deer engaged in coitus—an action that was condemned by all. To raise offspring, she forced his two wives to have offsprings from different gods.

In the *Mahabharata* none of the female characters had chosen her life mate by her own will. Satyavati did not choose Shantanu as a husband, nor did her daughters-in-law, Ambika and Ambalika. Gandhari was forced into marrying Dhritarashtra. Madri again did not become Pandu's wife of her own choice. Draupadi was won through a contest of skill and might—she did not personally pick out and choose Arjuna in her svayamvara. Uttara was offered to Arjuna as a wife, but he accepted her as his daughter-in-law, more on moral grounds than any other, a choice which could very well have been against Uttara's desire, though the epic contains no echoes of her feelings against the choice. That is five generations of daughters-in-law coming to the Bharata family as queens.

On the other hand, besides Draupadi, Arjuna and Bhima got married to several women who never enjoyed the position of an official wife. Kunti was forced to beget her three children from different sperm donor gods, but never any day could she claim Karna, whom she begot from the sun god Surya wish her own wish, before her marriage. It is told, though Draupadi had five husbands, yet still she had infatuations towards Lord Krishna and and Karna, the so-called illegitimate brothers of Pandavas. But never she could she any day express her love to them.

All these myths show us how patriarchal our great epic *Mahabharata* is. In *Ramayana*, where sensibilities were categorically denied to women we find the sad controversial saga of Ahalya. She was the wife of the great sage Gautama. Enamoured by her astounding beauty, Indra, lord of the gods, disguised himself as Gautama and approached Ahalya. During the middle of her sexual activity, she recognised the disguised Indra but she did not want to disturb her sexual bliss. So she played along and granted him sexual favours for which later she was punished and cursed to become a stone.

Never in our epics is there any sympathy regarding the denial of sexual rights of women; they were and always used for bearing offspring, males enjoyed sexual freedom over females. When a male writer writes about his sexual desire, passions or describes how many women he had craved for, the topic does not bring into question his moral integrity because they are sanctioned liberty to talk about sexuality. Salman Rushdie wedded his fifth love, and nobody pointed a finger at him but when Kamala Das became Kamala Surraiyah, the Indian society took it as a great social offence.[1]

Let us again return to our mythological values. Kunti suffered a lot for her illegitimate son Karna, but no one blamed the god Surya for this happening. Draupadi was insulted in the court of Kauravas, for having five the husbands at a time. Nobody blamed the Pandavas when they all jointly married a woman. They were even praised for obeying their mother's words, which were spoken inadvertently. Sex has different impact with gender variation. But in India, anything related to gender and sexuality in general is regarded as a forbidden topic. I have never read till now any comparison between male and female sexuality in Indian language. The penis is well suited for this role, projecting free from the body, but the vagina is itself an inner part of the body constituting a hidden mystic concern always for boys as well as for girls also. A girl is considered a minor until she has her first menstruation, but once she has it, she becomes an adult. These appropriations of social values do not concern a boy. Still after his puberty, he is considered as a minor and there is no firm rule or criteria when he should be considered as an adult. It is not shameful for a male to look at the body of a female with sensuous eyes; on the contrary, it is the female who bears the shame when a male looks at her. If a young male expresses his sensual pleasure to his peers in such a situation, they would share his pleasure. But if a girl expresses pleasure at seeing a male's physical features, her girlfriends would criticise her for being shameless. When a teen couple are found in a love affair and if a society has to condemn it, then the boy always gets excused for his adolescence and the girl is blamed for trapping the boy. Thus love plays a different role in the masculine and the feminine world. Once Simone wrote : "Man's love is of man's life a thing apart. This woman's whole existence".[2]

Sex is more related to emotion in the case of female whereas in males it does not always relate to any psychological bonding. This bonding in love is more important for women than it is for men, because men grow up with a sense of identity that exceeds the boundaries of family life, and bursts out with the recognition of the vast world outside, the taste for freedom, and the exploration of sexuality. Women are raised within the confinement of their homes and from their childhood it is taught to them that they have to be physically appealing in order to attract men, and finding a man to build a family around is mthe main mission in a woman's life.

I am not arguing against any love between two sexes. Unlike Simone, I always feel that women are 'other' than male with their biological, social and psychological differences. They have complete different sensibilities and different emotional spheres But, my point is this patriarchal society always tries to reject women's sensibility towards love The patriarchal concept of love between a man and woman actually means, how it is politicised, how it is socially and culturally manipulated with masculine view which is constructed by the idea of how to love a man, and how to care for him not only by our instinct, but by the socially expected gender roles. Social needs to sustain families on specifically prescribed gender roles also instruct us on how to love a man. There is a hidden code to exploit women in the whole cultural and social scheme of romantic love, mostly because the concept of romantic love has been authored by men, and is based on men's fractured understanding of women as primarily sexual objects. The patriarchal concept always denies the individuality of a woman as a human being.

For me love is a total submission from two sides, irrespective of any gender role. In this context, I want to again bring Simone as my example. The sex relation between Sartre and Simone was cool enough[3] and they had developed a relationship between Sartre, Simone and Sartre's student, Olga Kosakiewicz. Simone had her own bisexual relations and so did Sartre have many heterosexual relations; nobody showed any hostility to these relationships. Despite her relationship with Sartre, she had a love affair with, the American novelist, Nelson Algren; still they both maintained there relationship till Sartre's death.

Marxism was not a matter of faith or trust for Simone, it was a compulsion made by Sartre only. Without being related to the 'root' of the theory in her heart, we find Simone moving in the communes or in the Arab lands with Sartre, the 'last Sartre' bringing more confusion to the readers. On Monday, 19 July '48, Simone wrote to Algren. in her letter:

> If I could give up my life with Sartre I would be a dirty creature a treacherous and selfish woman... it is not by lack of love that I don't stay with you... Sartre needs me. In fact, he is very lonely, very tormented inside himself and I am his only true friend, I could not desert him... it is not possible to love more than I love you, flesh and heart and soul, but Sartre needs me.[4]

Like anger, fear, hatred, humour, love is also an emotion. This emotion, however, is different from other emotions because material elements like marriage, childbirth, divorce, dating, etc., build up upon this emotion to give a person's life a definite direction and shape. Love is the only emotion that channels itself into paving a path for our life. It is an integral complementarity for men and women, rather than the superiority of men over women or women over men. It is the sharing-ness of emotions and of life. I think it's more important to be a complete human being than be a writer, or a feminist or any other label one may be known by, but I also realise the reciprocal nature of living and writing. I believe that living gives you material (pleasure, pain, angst, loneliness, joy and what not) for writing, while writing helps you interpret your existence in a meaningful way. I live, I write, I grow and live some more and write some more and hopefully grow some more... That's my theory!

References

1. Krishnakumar, R. "A saffron offensive". *Frontline*, Volume 19 - Issue 24, November 23- December, 2002.
2. Actually, "'Man's love is of man's life a thing apart, / 'Tis woman's whole existence" is a Byron's line from his poem "Don Juan: Canto I : CXCIV" and Simone De Beauvoire has quoted it in her book *The Second Sex.*
3. Beauvoir, Simone de, *Wartime Diary,* University of Illinois Press, 2008.
4. Beauvoir, Simone de, *A Transatlantic Love Affair: Letters to Nelson Algren.* New Press August 1998. (Simone de Beauvoir met Nelson Algren in Chicago in February 1947, when a mutual friend arranged for him to serve as her tour guide for two days. The attraction was immediate, and within two months they were in love. Because Algren was so alien to de Beauvoir's world, she spent time describing events and people to him she might otherwise have taken for granted. The result is that de Beauvoir's 300 surviving letters to Algren are unusually rich in detail—love letters with a conscious undercurrent of French social history. The book is a posthumous publication.)

23 The Gate

An erotic book of Kafka was recently discovered from a British Library in London and at the Bodleian Library (Oxford University) by James Hawes, the academic and Kafka expert. Hawes revealed some of this erotic material in *Excavating Kafka*[1], published by Dr Franz Blei. Blei was the man who first published Kafka in 1908, with *Meditation*, a series of miniature stories later gathered in his book, according to the Friday, August 15 2008 edition of *The Guardian*.

****

Czech-born German-speaking Franz Kafka is considered the father of modern fiction, and his posthumously published novels and short stories like *The Metamorphosis*, *The Castle* and *The Trial* are treated as modern classics in the global literature. A common theme in those works is the alienation of the twentieth century man.

He was born no July 3, 1883 into a middle-class family in Prague, the capital of Bohemia, a kingdom then part of the Austro-Hungarian Empire. He grew up in an atmosphere of familial tensions and social rejection that he experienced as a member of Prague's Jewish minority. His attitude to his Jewish heritage was ambivalent. In a diary he wrote: "What have I in common with Jews? I have hardly anything in common with myself and should stand very quietly in a corner, content that I can breathe."[2]

Kafka was the eldest of six children. He had two younger brothers, George and Heinrich (who died at the ages of fifteen months and six months, respectively) and three younger sisters, Gabriele ("Elli") (1889–1941), Valerie ("Valli") (1890–1942), and Ottilie ("Ottla") (1892–1943). Ottilie was sent to the concentration camp and died there.

****

In Kafka's *The Trial*, the three major points of the novel are found in the ninth chapter:

1) One has to enter through the gate.
2) The gate is forbidden for him
3) The gate is only meant for him.

The novel is about a countryman who comes to appear before the law and he is not allowed to enter. The gatekeeper tells him, "If it tempts you so much, try it in spite of my prohibition. But take note: I am powerful. And I am only the lowliest gatekeeper. But from room to room stand gatekeepers, each more powerful than the other. I can't endure even one glimpse of the third."

The man from the country has not expected such difficulties. He thinks the law should always be accessible for everyone, but as he now looks more closely at the gatekeeper in his fur coat, at his large pointed nose and his long, thin, black Tartar's beard, he decides that it would be better to wait until he gets permission to go inside. The gatekeeper gives him a stool and allows him to sit down at the side in front of the gate.

There he sits for days and years. He makes many attempts to be let in, and he wears the gatekeeper out with his requests. The gatekeeper often interrogates him briefly, questioning him about his homeland and many other things. But they are indifferent questions, the kind great men put, and at the end, he always tells him once more that he cannot let him inside yet. The man, who has equipped himself with many things for his journey, spends everything, no matter how valuable, to win over the gatekeeper. The latter takes it all but, as he does so, says, "I am taking this only so that you do not think you have failed to do anything."

During the many years the man observes the gatekeeper almost continuously. He forgets the other gatekeepers, and this one seems to him the only obstacle for entry into the law. He curses the unlucky circumstance—in the first years, thoughtlessly and out loud and as he grows old, mumbling to himself. He becomes childish and, since in the long years studying the gatekeeper he has come to know the fleas in his fur collar, he even asks the fleas to help him persuade the gatekeeper. Finally his eyesight grows weak and he does not know whether things are really darker around him or whether his eyes are merely deceiving him. But he recognises now, in the darkness, an illumination which breaks inextinguishably out of the gateway to the law. Now he no longer has much time to live. Before his death, he gathers in his head all his experiences of the entire time up into one question which he has not yet put to the gatekeeper. He waves to him, since he can no longer lift up his stiffening body. The gatekeeper has to bend way down to him, for the great difference has changed things to the disadvantage of the man.

"What do you still want to know, then?" the gatekeeper inquires. "You are insatiable."

"Everyone strives after the law," says the man. "So how is that in these many years, no one except me has requested entry?"

The gatekeeper sees that the man is already dying and in order to reach his diminishing sense of hearing, he shouts at him, "Here no one else can gain entry since this entrance was assigned only to you. I'm going now to close it."

****

Away from conventional critical appreciation that the 'gate' is a symbol of religion and God, let us think of another alternative. What else can this 'gate' and 'gatekeepers' stand for?

It is said that Kafka had many girlfriends, many affairs, and a number of broken engagements. During 1911 and 1912, he was attracted to Flora Klug and Mania Tschissik, both actresses in the Prague Jewish Theatre. On August 13, 1912, he met Felice Bauer, a 24-year-old businesswoman from Berlin. Their relationship lasted for five years. Felice later moved to the United States, where she died in 1960.

In August 1917, Kafka discovered that he had contracted tuberculosis, and during his treatment, he fell in love with a woman named Milena Jesenská, a 24-year-old writer who had translated some of his stories into Czech. Kafka's fear of sexuality was probably the main reason for his decision to leave Milena. In 1913, he wrote in his diary *Der Coitus als Bestrafung des Glückes des Beisammenseins* [The Coitus as punishment of the luck of the gathering] and in the winter of 1920-21, he stopped sending her regular letters. After they separated, she worked as a journalist and died in a German concentration camp in 1944. After their relationship ended, Kafka wrote his last novel, *The Castle*, where 'K', the protagonist of the novel. arrives at a village, claiming to be a land surveyor.[3]

In January, 1919, Kafka met Julie Wohryzek in the Italian Tyrol. It was a short-term relationship and perhaps Kafka lost his interest but interestingly enough, he may have enjoyed a brief physical relationship unlike his other relationships. Kafka also enjoyed a brief loving friendship with Minze Eisner before he met Dora Diamant, a 25-year-old woman from an Orthodox Jewish family who worked in the kitchen of a holiday camp in 1922. In 1924, Kafka moved with Dora to the Kierling Sanatorium outside Vienna. When he wrote to Dora's father and proposed marriage to Dora, the reply was "no." Kafka died of tuberculosis on June 3, 1924. However,

Dora later described herself as "the wife of Franz Kafka." She died in London in 1952.

Throughout his life, we observe Kafka's deep feelings towards his girlfriends as well as his concerns about their suitability as married partners. We also observe his growing fears about his health, and most important, we observe his decision to place the discipline of his art above his hopes for personal happiness.

****

Die Verwandlung (The Metamorphosis) was the short story with which Kafka's first creative period started. In this story, the protagonist, Gregor Samsa, awoke from uneasy dreams to find that he had turned, overnight, into a giant insect. He remained trapped in his room by his petit bourgeois family. His father threw an apple core at Gregor and Gregor died. As the protagonist spent more time as an insect, he began to heal at an accelerated rate. "Am I less sensitive now?" he asks. Gregor virtually felt himself alienated and lonely. If Prufrock was T.S. Eliot, it is also fair to say that Gregor Samsa was Kafka, who was basically a giant consumptive insect in a world of strangers.

His mother's intentions from the beginning appeared to be more concerned for her financial support than Gregor's happiness. His sister was very close to him and was the only member of the family who truly only cared about his happiness or well-being. She was the only member of the family who brought him food or ventured into his room after his metamorphosis. She even took care to notice what foods particularly liked and brought more of the same for him.

We once again see the significance of a picture when Gregor's mother and sister begin moving things from his room to accommodate his new shape Gregor becomes enraged, as he does not want to completely give up his old life and is torn between his new desires and the good memories of his life. The one item in his room that he decides to keep is his picture of a woman in a fur coat. His mother and sister are trying to move the picture, by distancing him from his personal feelings. Gregor chooses to make a stand on that which represents his effeminacy. He displays his sexuality and his mother witnesses it, much to her shock and dismay. Gregor's father returns to find his wife passed out and becomes enraged at Gregor. Gregor marvels at how different his father seems now than before his metamorphosis: "And yet, and yet, could that be his father?"

****

Kafka's relationship with those close to him has always remained under suspicion and through his physical intimacy with other gender (say Gregor's sister), it kept him away, mentally. This may be why Kafka didn't find any particular success with relationships in his love life. Unable to reconcile his physical urges with his romantic longings, he had a series of prolonged, probably chaste, engagements that invariably ended in his breaking off the relationship. It makes a clear distinctive reason that the 'suppressed libido' of Kafka may have caused him to write a porno book along with all the other masterpieces he created.

****

Kafka never visited the United States. But he wrote *Der Verschollene* (retitled *Amerika*), which was published as his posthumous unfinished novel in 1927. The protagonist of the novel is Karl Rossmann, a 17-year-old young adult. As he enters New York Harbour as an immigrant and sees the Statue of Liberty, he observes that she holds in her right hand not a lamp, but a sword. For Kafka, we can find a great resemblance between sexuality and America. He had never experienced these two, yet they both bothered him.

Notes and References

1. James Hawes, a British lecturer and satirical novelist, in his recent book *Excavating Kafka* bombed by revealing uncelebrated "erotica" stash kept in a locked boc'kshelf in the journal Amethyst (1905-1906), later retitled *Opals* (1907) by the eminent writer Franz Kafka. They're archived at the British Library and the Bodleian Library at Oxford. Kafka's erotica contains illustrations, some surreal or satirical in nature. One has a wiry skeleton reaching for a cowering miniature nude; another, a frog's mouth on a suggestively shaped plant.

   The journal *Amethyst/ Opals* was privately published and was available only via subscription in numbered, limited editions. It included reprints of material by Goethe, illustrations by artists like Aubrey Beardsley, and reprinted and newly translated erotic prose from old and recent Turkish, Indian, French, English and Italian texts, including writing by Casanova, Wilde, Rimbaud, Keats and the symbolist poet Verlaine. There was also cutting-edge fiction, like the debut of a seminal Expressionist novel, *Bebuquin* by Carl Einstein. Interestingly enough Kafka's friend Max Brod, who later ignoring Kafka's wishes to burn his work, published them and helped establish Kafka as a legend, was also a contributor to that journal. It is also another interesting fact that Franz Blei, the publisher of that erotic journal was the first publisher of Kafka.

   Kafka was not very interested with *Amethyst / Opals* and in one of his letter to Max Brod, he once wrote to split the cost of an expensive subscription to *Amethyst*, though he doesn't go into detail about what that means. Max Brod mentioned that Kafka could never get to read more than a line of two of *Casanova* because according to Kafka the novel was dirty, immoral seemed to have no attraction for him.

   These all facts may make the readers confused, but Mr. Hawes writes, "Things get far simpler if we forget the icon and, for once, just try to treat Kafka as a normal human being." (Hawes, James. *Excavating Kafka.* Quercus Publishing Plc, 2008,)

2. These diaries reveal the essential Kafka behind the enigmatic artist. Covering the period from 1910 to 1923, the year before Kafka's death at the age of forty, they provide a penetrating look into Kafka's world—notes on life in Prague, accounts of his dreams, his feelings for the father he worshipped and for the woman he could not bring himself to marry, his sense of guilt and of being an outcast, and his struggles and triumphs in expressing himself as a writer.

Kafka left instructions with Max Brod to burn all of these journals. Max, however, believed they were too important to be lost and devoted himself to organising the diaries for publication. Kafka made his entries in a manner convenient for himself: starting at the back, writing upside down, changing journals daily. All of this made the task of organising them very difficult. Max Brod did a tremendous job and only misjudged the placement of a handful of entries. The diaries themselves contain a lot of things no writer would want seen. They are fragments, drafts, and sketches he worked on during the nights. Most are not very good—as they are. Their value comes in the later, published, incarnations. These writings give us a little insight into the way Franz Kafka worked. Several of the entries are worked and reworked over a period of years. They show subtle shifts in his insight, perspective, and craftsmanship. (See: Kafka, Franz. *The Diaries of Franz Kafka.* Schocken; Schocken; 1988,)

3. Stach, Reiner, *Kafka: The Decisive Years,* Harcourt, 2005.

24 Forbidden Desires

While writing my article on Kafka's book, my American poet /painter friend, Ed Baker, advised me not to use the word 'porn' but to use 'erotica' instead. So this will be the theme of this article: porn v. erotica.

For many, the topic of sex still remains a 'forbidden text' and I have noticed readers feel hesitant to make their comments on it. Those who are not hesitant have posted comments on my last article and I thank them for their responses. How societal we are!

Alan Moore: Comic Book Author or Pornographer?

British writer Alan Moore (born November 18, 1953) is one of the most critically acclaimed authors in the field of comic books. Besides his novel *Voice of the Fire*, Moore has written comic books like *Watchmen*, *V for Vendetta*, and *From Hell*. He brings a wide range of influences among other writers. In his student life, Moore was expelled from school for dealing LSD. He wrote and drew underground-style strips for music magazines, including *Sounds* and the *NME*. Under the pseudonyms Curt Vile and Jill de Ray (an alternative spelling of the serial killer Gilles de Rais), he began a weekly strip, "Maxwell the Magic Cat," for the *Northants Post* newspaper.

In 2006, he published an eight-page article tracing out the history of pornography and argued that a society's vibrancy and success are related to its permissiveness in sexual matters.

In 1992-93, he published few chapters of his novel *Lost Girls*[1] and in 2009 the novel has been released in book form1. It is a graphic novel, which includes some graphic presentations of Moore's girlfriend Melinda Gebbie.

Gebbie, a graphic designer and Moore's girlfriend, told, in an interview with Matt Singer, that "this was going to be pornography for women or it wasn't worth doing. Women like a sense of aesthetics in pornography. They don't like looking at females who are cold and abused and unhappy. That's what they see looking at them from just about every porn image."[2]

Lost Girls describes the sexual fantasies of three important female fictional characters of the late nineteenth and early twentieth century: 'Alice' from *Alice's Adventures in Wonderland,*[3] 'Dorothy Gale' from *The Wizard of Oz*[4], and 'Wendy Darling' from *Peter Pan.*[5] The three women are separately on holiday at an expensive mountain resort hotel in Austria on the eve of World War I (1913–1914). Alice is now a gray-haired old woman named "Lady Fairchild." Dorothy is now in her 20s. And Wendy is in her 30s and married to a man named Harold Potter who is 20 years her senior. The women meet by chance and begin to exchange erotic stories from their pasts.

Moore on Porn

Alan Moore has described this work as 'pornography.' While talking to Kurt Amacker,[6] and Daniel Robert Epstein,[7] he never uttered the word 'erotica' but always claimed the novel as 'pornography' or 'sex comedy.'

And in an interview with Noel Murray, the author further related "...though probably the Victorian erotica played a bigger part than the estimable Robert Crumb. I looked at a relatively small amount of contemporary erotica and found that it didn't really appeal. None of the filmed or photographic material did anything for me because there's such a lot of emotional human baggage that comes with anything that involves real models, real actors. You're too aware that this is somebody real, and that they might not have actually wanted to do this for a living. There's an air of disappointment or sadness that hangs over the material. So I tended to gravitate toward literary and artistic pornography of the Victorian and Edwardian period, simply because it's a lot better. It was a kind of golden age of porn."

In that interview with Kurt Amacker, the author said, "I know that there has been sort of an argument that, 'Oh, well, pornography causes rape' because most rapists have read pornography at some point in their lives. I should imagine that they've also drunk milk. But, whether there's a direct connection, I doubt it. And it has to be said that in countries where they have a more liberal approach to pornography, such as Denmark or Holland, that they have far, far less raped and murdered children thrown into the canal as we do over here in England."

And in an interview with Pádraig Ó Méalóid[8], the author said, "If we'd have come out and said, 'well, this is a work of art,' they would have probably all said, 'no it's not; it's pornography.' So because we're saying, 'this is pornography,' they're saying, 'no it's not; it's art,' and people don't realise quite what they've said."

What's in a Word?

What then, is the difference between 'erotica' and 'porn?' This question has been discussed many times, and still has not been completely answered. A majority of the people though still consider either erotica or porn as their 'private matter' and show reluctance to make it 'social' subject.

When the' Nudist movement' started in Germany in the early twentieth century, it was advocated that that it was associated with the concepts of 'returning to nature' and 'creating equality.'[9] That idea of naturalism in nudity later spread to England, Canada, the United States, and beyond where a network of clubs developed. Now clothes-free beaches and other types of anonymous nudist activities have been adopted by many with an idea to promote 'tourist naturism.'

Nudity: What is it, Really?

For centuries, nudity has been one of the most common art subjects. In art, being naked and nudity are not same. It is interesting to note that in all our art forms, only female nudity and never masculine nudity has been considered as any form of artistic milieu. A few years back, Saroj Bal, an Oriya writer and editor, published his own nude picture in a self-edited magazine in India and it created a controversy.[10] So, it cannot be denied that there seems to be an automatic association with the current concept of nudity in art and patriarchal values.

But in ancient art forms, especially in Greek art and in Hindu sculptures found on temple walls, we find masculine nudity to be a common feature. But still the question remains unsolved: What is the difference between an artistic nude and someone being naked? Can we count a *Playboy* centrefold as a nude or a painting of Aphrodite as naked? I think an artistic nude is a portrait of someone who is untouchable and unattainable. And for this reason, pictures of naked Greek gods and goddesses or Hindu sculptures on temple walls are not counted under the guise of naked portraiture. That means nudity is a far away concept from our lives, as conventional patriarchal society has adopted and fixed it as a universal norm.

Someone once wrote (I forgot who) that most of the time, 'erotica' has explicit sex scenes and portrays sex in a positive light. For us, we want erotica that is story-driven, although the story doesn't necessarily have to be a romance. Sex must be in a positive light and between consenting adults. Porn isn't about being sensual nor is it erotic. On the contrary, 'porn' is all about instant, sexual gratification, and is often derogatory and demeaning toward women.

But defining these differences remains difficult. What will be the criteria to decide the 'positive light?' Subjective attitudes make it more complicated. Why won't we refer to *Kama Sutra* as porn rather than erotica when there are no dealings with the human heart and soul in the text? In that historically widely accepted book Vatsyayan, the author, has divided women in four groups with respect to sexuality. Why doesn't the author categorise men with their sexuality? Where do we find 'sexual gratification' towards woman?

There are many examples in our myths where we find erotica is placed on the same plane with spiritualism. Lord Krishna is considered as one of the incarnations of Lord Vishnu. In *Bhagavad Purana*, Lord Krishna had stolen the clothes of the Gopis (the women of Gopa Pura) while they are bathing in the river Yamuna, leaving them naked. This stealing of the Gopis' clothing is treated as a highly devotional phenomenon and has inspired many of the medieval poets of Bhakti Yuga. Krishna had also performed Rasa Lila or cosmic dances with 16,000 Gopis, making love to each of the women individually. These activities are never treated as 'porno' in Hindu society. But Hindu society shows its reluctant intolerance towards modern erotica. I think this is the most amazing contradiction of our time.

If I have to admire the Shringar poems of medieval Hindu poets, I will appreciate Jaydev even more because in no sense did he paint sexuality with gender inclination. He painted lust, the passion, and the love of both male and female. And he was not afraid to write a masculine character, Krishna, saying to his lover fiancé Radha, "Dehi pada pallav mudaram (your foot on my head—a sublime flower destroying the poison of love)." I can say this one may be erotic, as here, we find somehow the masculine dominancy over human love is denied.

And in Closing...

It is interesting to note Radclyffe Hall's *Well of Loneliness*[11] has been declared as obscene and pornographic. I have never found any sexually explicit descriptions or the so-called 'obscene words' in that book. Nowadays, it is unbelievable to think that 80-90 years ago, the author was taken to court.[12]

I am never a supporter of 'porno' and I always believe that it makes woman a 'product', always associated with male-dominant consumerism. But it is also true that every sexually explicit topic is not 'porno.' I would be happier if Alan Moore would have used the word 'erotica' instead of 'porno' for his novel *Lost Girls*.

Notes and References

1. "Lost Girls" is Alan Moore's ambitious 280 page intellectual 'porn' (erotic or 'porn'?) fantasy graphic novel, starring Wendy (of *Peter Pan*), Dorothy (of *Wizard of Oz*) and Alice (of *Alice's Adventures in Wonderland*). Illustrated by his girlfriend, underground artist Melinda Gebbie., published by Top Shelf Productions, 2006.

   Generally feminists oppose pornography. But, interestingly enough, I haven't read any criticism of *Lost Girls* from a feminist's pen.
2. Singer, Matt, "A talk with Lost Girls artist Melinda Gebbie": *The Village Voice,* alternative weekly of New York times since 1955, Tuesday, August 15 2006
3. *Alice's Adventures in Wonderland* (1865) is a novel written by English author Charles Lutwidge Dodgson under the pseudonym Lewis Carroll. It tells the story of a girl named Alice who falls down a rabbit-hole into a fantasy world populated by peculiar and anthropomorphic creatures. (See: Carroll, Lewis, *Alice's Adventures in Wonderland*, HarperCollins, 1992.
4. *The Wonderful Wizard of Oz* is a children's novel written by L. Frank Baum and illustrated by W.W. Denslow. It tells the adventures of a girl named Dorothy in the Land of Oz in the year 1889. (See: Baum, L. Frank, *The Wonderful Wizard of Oz*, HarperCollins; 2000.
5. The book *Peter Pan* by J. M. Barrie is truly a children's book worth reading for adults. Peter Pan is mischievous boy who can fly and magically refuses to grow up, spends his never-ending childhood adventuring on the small island of Never Land. Wendy is his girl friend. The novel was first published in 1902. See: Barrie, J. M., *Peter Pan*, Harper Festival, 2003.

6. The interview appeared in Online Magazine *Mania* on April 12, 2006.
7. The interview appeared in Online magazine "Majory.Com" on June 7, 2006.
8. The interview appeared in Online magazine "Forbidden Planet" on June 13, 2008.
9. Ross, Chad: *Naked Germany: Health, Race, and the Nation*, Berg Publishers, New York, 2005.
10. The nude picture of the editor Saroj Bal was appeared in the Oriya Magazine *Galpa Patrika* in its 2006 Puja Special issue.
11. Hall, Radclyffe, *The Well of Loneliness*, Knopf Doubleday Publishing Group, reprent publication 1990, pp. 437.
12. When the English writer Radclyffe Hall's (1880-1943) book, *The Well of Loneliness*, was published in London, even though the book lacked a single sex scene authorities declared it obscene and seized it. In a New York court, the presiding judge ruled that the book "tends to debauch public morals," and found the publisher guilty, but on appeal, the charge was dismissed.

25 The Myriad of Molly Blooms

At the very beginning of James Joyce's *Ulysses*, Molly Bloom, the cuckolding wife of Leopold Bloom, appears to the readers as a common Irish lady of the twentieth century. But in the 60 pages of scandalous, scatological, sarcastic and disturbingly profound monologue that follow, she appears as a sex monster, a lusty, lewd, outspoken, witty, and self-aware woman, seducing young boys even though she is a married woman.

Molly's frustration is being a married woman in a marriage that lacks the sexual freedom she needs. She fantasizes about her sexual desires and dreams because it is a human quality that she is not willing to suppress. And she makes no apologies for it. Some critics appreciate Joyce's characterisation of Molly as a step forward to paint a free woman in Western literature

Joyce and Feminism

Richard Brown, the author of *James Joyce and Sexuality*, writes: "Joyce constructed out of his own version of feminist literary tradition and its obtrusive sexual dimorphism is conceived as a vindication of, rather than an attack on, femininity."[1] Brown found "obscured the relationship between contemporary feminism and his success."[2] He added an interesting discussion of "sexual dimorphism."[3] In support of his idea, he stated that for Bloom, the world is "full of analogies to sexual difference."[4] Brown sees Joyce as depending heavily upon a "strong sense" of difference between the sexes, using "Penelope" as an example of Joyce creating the "separate female character."[5] He does not see Joyce's portrayal of Molly and other female characters through the eyes of men as misogynistic, since many of the male characters "suffer the same fate" when seen through women's eyes, such as Bloom and Boylan. Brown concluded his discussion with a confirmatory tone that Joyce constructed Molly out of his "own version of feminist literary tradition and its obtrusive sexual dimorphism is conceived as a vindication of, rather than attack on, femininity."[6]

Declan Kiberd writes in his Introduction to the 1992 Penguin edition of *Ulysses*, that Joyce ponders a life spent fitting pins into hair and clothing, or making adjustments to disorderly skirts under the protective coverage of a friend in the street. His fellow-feeling for women in the momentous labour of childbirth is accompanied by a similar empathy with the woman suddenly being taken short in a city whose lavatories, like its pubs, were notoriously built for men only. This empathy is nowhere clearer than in Bloom's attitude to women who are caught in moments of disadvantage.[7]

Can Joyce be reclaimed for feminism? Suzette Henke tries to find psychoanalytical answers with the ideas of Freud, Lacan and Kristeva. She argues that Joyce invokes gender stereotypes in order to "mock and subvert traditional notions" of gender, focusing on constructions of the "gendered subject" and touching on ideas of androgyny, bisexual fantasy, and motherhood. She discusses Molly's monologue as "steeped" in the languages of Edwardian pornography and "Victorian sentimental fiction."[3]

No doubt, Joyce was the prime figure to bring erotic sexuality to English Literature, and his experiments were not with writings, but with lives and people as well. His constant visits to prostitutes, his experiments with verbal sex, and persuasion to Nora for her active participations are examples of how Joyce gave importance of sexuality in his life and writings.

Brenda Maddox writes in her book *Nora: A Biography of Nora Joyce* that Joyce was amazed at female sexuality when on his first date with Nora, she "unbuttoned his trousers, slipped in her hand, pushed his shirt aside and, acting with some skill (according to his later account), made him a man."[9]

Nora: A Biography of Nora Joyce (1988) tells us that Joyce made Molly Bloom the prototype of his wife Nora. A reporter once asked Nora if she was actually Molly Bloom from *Ulysses*. She replied, "I'm not—she was much fatter."

Nora: A Woman /A Character

Nora Barnacle met Joyce on June 10, 1904, but it was not until June 16, 1904 that they had their first romantic liaison. After only three months dating, they flew away to Trieste (at that time in Austria-Hungary) but they did not marry. Meanwhile, Nora gave birth to her first son Giorgio on June 27, 1905 and later to a daughter, Lucia, in July 26. A miscarriage in 1908 coincided with the beginning of a series of difficulties for Nora, which placed a strain on her relationship with Joyce and made it increasingly conflicted. After 27 years of living together relationship, at last, they got married in 1931.

Nora and Joyce did not have a very happy life. Though at the beginning, they at least had very sensual romantic lives, later on, they remained in tension and Nora was often complaining about Joyce as a weak man and a neurotic artist. In her letters to her sister, Nora accuses Joyce of ruining her life and that of their children. She says he drinks too much and wastes too much money. As for his literary activity, she laments the fact that his writings are obscure and lacking in sense. She hates attending his meetings with other artists and admits she would have preferred him had he been a musician rather than a writer. Their marital life became hell when their daughter Lucia went mad and son Giorgio left for America after marrying an American lady.

Before Joyce, Nora had only three affairs in her teenage years. She fell in love with a teenager named Michael Feeney, who died soon after of typhoid and pneumonia. In a dramatic but unrelated coincidence, her second lover died in 1900, garnering her the name of "man-killer" from her friends. It was rumoured that she sought solace from her friend, budding English theatre starlet, Laura London, who also introduced her to a Protestant named Willie Mulvagh. In 1903, she was sent away after her uncle learned of the affair and dubious friendship. In a later period, besides Joyce, Nora had no other relationship as Molly Bloom had, but Joyce was always suspicious with the thought that Nora might have been unfaithful to him. Joyce thus had in his mind a strong link between Nora's sexual allure and death (because two of her teenage fiancés' death), and he focused on this morbid love theme in poems such as "She Weeps over Rahoon" and his best-known short story from the *Dubliners*, "The Dead."

So, we don't find any similarities between Molly Bloom and Nora if we overrule the three of teenage love relations she had. It may be fact that Nora became pregnant through Joyce at her first dating, but that was not a proof of her infidelities.

Is Molly a Free Woman ?

Molly is a woman who knows what drives a man crazy and how to seduce him at the drop of a hat. Even though she is a married woman, she does not forget how to seduce men because she has the frustration of being a married woman in a marriage that lacks the sexual connection she wants. She not only does it but needs the art of fantasy because it is a human quality that she is not willing to suppress. She fantasizes and makes no apologies for it. It shows that she is a rebellious by nature. But is she a free woman actually?

If Molly were truly sexually free, she would not go to church for confession of her guilt. She feels regrets about her infidelities and blames Leopold. "It's his own fault if I am an adulteress," she says. If she were a free woman, she would not give Leopold the credit for turning her in to an "adulteress," nor would she use the word "adulteress" because that word has a very negative connotation which implies guilt and shame. If Molly were a free woman, she would not feel terrible about the infidelity and the betrayal to her husband. She invokes God for creating Eve as the first sin of the Creator. By invoking that religious belief, she subconsciously proves the classic notion of patriarchal ideas that women are sinful by nature. If she had been guilt-free of affairs, she would have invoked poetry, pagan goddesses, humanly body pleasure, but not the creation of woman by God.

Molly also refers to one of Leopold's pen pal as a "little bitch." Molly Bloom's jealousy of her husband's infidelities and her anger toward Leopold are also indications that she is deeply hurt by their failing relationship and lack of sex.

Actually, Molly represents the common European female characteristics of that time, which the contemporary writings lack. As a very common woman, Molly is also tied down to the fears of aging and losing her sex appeal, which she manifests in her fantasies about seducing Stephen. She is not actually craving for sex, but rather, an emotional bonding. "I wish somebody would write me a love letter", she cries, showing her desperation for a lover who will fulfil her emotional needs.

Was Nora Really Molly Bloom?

It is difficult to say whether or not Nora was the Molly Bloom of *Ulysses* because except for the three premature affairs as a teenager, Nora sticks to her relationship with Joyce. But Joyce had a double-standard on women's sexuality. Joyce was traditionally masculine in terms of sexual jealousy, possessiveness, and stereotyping of his 'love.' He was extremely jealous of Nora's fondness for anyone but himself, including her own father and children. As Maddox puts it,

Joyce "could tolerate no thought of a rival for Nora's affections,"[10] and he felt irrationally betrayed that her cousins could co-exist with her love for him.

When courting Nora the summer of 1904, Joyce began to become possessive, and his jealousy revealed his insecurity. According to Maddox, "As the summer wore on, and he became more and more attached to Nora. Joyce showed the first signs of suspiciousness. She had three free evenings in a row that he could not account for."[11] Sexually, Joyce held Nora to a double standard; though he had consorted with prostitutes and had at least one "bout of venereal disease"[12] prior to meeting Nora, "doubt continued to torment Joyce"[13] about whether Nora had been a virgin or not before having sexual intercourse with him. He could not stand the thought of her having been with another man, even before she met him. As Maddox states, "Joyce never conquered his fear of Nora's old loves,"[14] which is why her old Galway beaus, such as Willie Mulvagh, had their names and/or actions immortalised in the obsessiveness of Joyce's writing.

J. Mays relates how while visiting Dublin without Nora in 1909, Joyce "became obsessed with the thought that Nora might have been unfaithful to him" with Vincent Cosgrave.[15] This obsession made its way into Joyce's poetry, his play *Exiles*, and *Ulysses*, not to mention some raving and accusatorial letters to Nora. Joyce was quick to believe Cosgrave's words about his sexual relations with Nora before even hearing Nora's version of events, and it took the word of two males, Joyce's friend J. F. Byrne (the model for Cranly in *A Portrait of the Artist as a Young Man*) and his brother Stanislaus, to convince him that Cosgrave had lied to him about Nora.[16]

Even so, he remained so suspicious and bitterly jealous of Cosgrave, his former friend and possible precursor of Nora's affections, that he lampooned and abused him as Lynch in *Ulysses,* and enjoyed hearing about his early demise and unsuccessful career.[17] None of this is the behaviour of a man who really believes in free love and open relationships. Nora's experimental enthusiasm for sex and, as Brenda Maddox's book explains, the fact "that Nora could release such fervour only three weeks after initiation left him with a lasting sense of awe at the banked fires of female desire."[18]

Why did Joyce Metamorphose Nora into Molly Bloom?

Art is not what you see but what you make others see. What is important is how one views life as a whole and hence, the reader's psyche has indeed a lot to do with how the work is interpreted. I don't blame Joyce, as some feminist critics did, for being unjust to Nora. Writing is a totally difficult and complex process. An author has to make himself/herself a multi-winged personality—one goes above the surroundings and canvas so that the author him/herself can observe everything with full objectivity. Another enters into the character. And the third one assimilates an author's self with the character.

So, when Joyce tries to paint Molly in *Ulysses* and *Bertha in Exiles*, we find not the Nora, but the Joyce with his 'manly woman' personality. As Richard Brown explains about Molly, she "surely does represent a new kind of fictional woman: massive, potent and self-possessed. Though few modern feminists have wished to avail themselves of that image of femininity, it was evidently one which Joyce constructed out of his own version of feminist literary tradition, and its obtrusive sexual dimorphism is conceived as a vindication of, rather than an attack on, femininity."[19]

I have no allegation against Joyce. Above all, I appreciate his feelings, as I am not only a feminist but a writer in my soul, always.

References

1. Brown, Richard; *James Joyce and Sexuality*, 1985, p. 101.
2. Ibid., p. 91.

3. Ibid., p. 96-97.
4. Ibid., p. 97.
5. Ibid., p. 98.
6. Ibid., p. 101.
7. Kiberd, Declan, *Introduction to the Penguin edition of Ulysses,* 1992, pp. iii-iv.
8. Henke, Suzette A. *James Joyce and the Politics of Desire*, New York: Routledge, 1990.
9. Maddox, Brenda, *Nora: A Biography of Nora Joyce,* 1988, p. 42.
10. Ibid., p. 23.
11. Ibid., p. 47.
12. Ibid., p. 48.
13. Ibid., p. 70.
14. Ibid., p. 131.
15. Mays, J., (Editor), *Poems and Exiles*, Penguin Books, London, p. xxxvi.
16. Maddox, Brenda, op.cit., p. 125.
17. Ibid., pp. 320-1.
18. Ibid., p. 79.
19. Brown, Richard, op.cit., p. 101.

26 The Changing Voices of Rebati Remain the Same

Rebati, a country girl of Orissa in India at the end of nineteenth century, had intended to read and learn more though she could manage to learn many devotional songs, the *bhajans* and could memorise the verses of *Bhagavad Gita*. Her father Shyambandhu Mohanty, a village tax collector for the local landlord zamindars arranged a private tutor, Basudev Mohapatra. This teacher, popularly known as Basu Master, was the only teacher of the village upper primary school. He graduated from Cuttack Normal School. Rebati's grandma was against such type of liberation to Rebati as she thought reading and writing were not meant for a girl. She should learn cooking, housekeeping, sewing or other skills which were meant for a girl. But Shyambandhu did not pay attention to his mother's complaints. During their tuition, a silent love affair developed between the teacher and the student although they did not express their feelings verbally. The story turned into a tragic mode when Shyambandhu and his wife died due to cholera one after another. The zamindar overthrew the facilities given to Shyambandhu and the family was in distress. As Basudev was the only male person closer to that family he came forward to take the responsibility of these two dismayed women. But perhaps God was more cruel than we thought and due to Basudev also died cholera, leaving Rebati and her grandma totally alone and without any support or shelter, while he was in a short tour to another examination. Adding to these serial deaths and other consequences, Rebati's grandma began to believe that these misfortunes were coming as a curse for Rebati's education. She blamed and began to rebuke Rebati for her unusual role of showing interest in male chores. Rebati was harassed, mentally broken after the death of her parents and of her lover mentor Basudev. She fell sick and at last died leaving her grandma lonely.

'Rebati'[1] is a landmark story in Indian fiction with many extraordinary and advanced qualities in comparison with other stories written at that time in India literature. It is the first story, written about middle class life. The stories of that time were most probably based on the royal family. It is a great story which dealt with feminism and especially with the rights for women's education.

Some queries and doubts have been asked by my students from time to time. How could it be possible for a ten-year old girl to find herself mentally involved with a grown-up man? Why did Shyambandhu not send her to school when there was an upper primary school in the village? In the story, all the supporters of women's education died while the grandma, who differed from them and was opposing female education, survived till the end of the story. Did Fakir Mohan want to send the message that girls' education was a fatal decision for society?

Rebati was only a ten-year-old girl. Assuming the present day situation, a ten-year-old girl was a mere child for either marriage or for love. But if we consider the nineteenth-century Indian culture, a ten-year-old girl is quite old enough for starting her young-age activities. The age of marriage for a girl-child had been set at ten years old in 1860; the Special Marriage Bill raised it to 14 years for Brahmos in 1872; and in 1891, the age was raised to 12 years for all girls. But reformers considered this to be barbarically low; and their attempts to raise the age of consent still further were seen by conservatives as an attack on Hindu culture.

The story was a unique presentation of social conditions in rural India. When contemporary readers try to imagine these conditions in comparison with those currently, it seems to them somehow unbelievable, impractical and impossible, though the conditions were prevailing at that time. These consequences and change in scenario proves the tremendous social changes in our social life in the last century only. In the eighteenth century, there was no standardised institutional education facility for young children in India. They were taught reading, writing of vernacular language, specially aimed with reading skill for all *Puranas* and *Shastras*, and perhaps a little arithmetic and Sanskrit. Reading and writing were not so mandatory for the girls, rather they were taught cooking, sewing, and household management; above all, education was a family responsibility, not a social obligation. The administration or the king's court had nothing to do with this education system.

Perhaps the best-known educational arrangement in pre-colonial India was lying in the hand of private tutors who opened 'village schools' (named as 'chahali', 'chatsala' or 'pathashala') and it was a traditional ancestral occupation for such teachers. A legal entitlement to standardised instruction for all children was first implemented by the British in the eighteenth century, and schools and colleges for vernacular and English education and even Madrassas for Arabic or Farsi education were established. But the girls' education still remained in a miserable condition as the middle class parents still did not like the idea of educating their girls with language or arithmetic. At the beginning of the nineteenth century, a British company started to educate the Indians and opened schools for children. In 1821, the Church Missionary Society of India decided to establish 30 schools for Hindu girls and Miss Mary Anne Cooke was asked to manage them. The first boarding school for girls was opened in Thirunelveli in this year. By1840, six schools with an enrolment of 200 Hindu girls were constructed.[2] Until the mid-nineteenth century, the

Church Missionary Society enrolled 8,000 girls under its banner. In 1871, a school for Hindu girls was setup at Cuttack and even after the school ran for ten years, the number of girls had increased by a mere 25.[3]

'Rebati' was written in 1898, where the protagonist's father employed a village master for his daughter's tuition at home. The story was not merely a love story as Rebati never asked for love from her mentor Basu Master. In the story, except a 'smile' the readers could not access any picturisation of love ideas.

Fakir Mohan was associated with the first girls' school of Orissa. When it was found that after ten years of establishing the school, only four Hindu girls were enrolled, Senapati was one of the persons who drew the attention of parents and urged them to send their girls to the school in larger numbers. But in his story, the family of Rebati has been ruined and her grandmother believed that this disaster could happen due to enforcing girls' education against tradition. Fakir Mohan was not an idealistic propagandist unlike other writers of his time. He didn't want to glamourise girls' education but tried to portray the idea of his contemporary society regarding this education.

Some critics try to project the central theme of the story confined to women's education. But really, it is the first Indian short story which deals with women's identity and sexuality. The female sexuality in the nineteenth century was oppressed by patriarchal society. Though the girls were married off at the age of 8-10, the age limit of their grooms was not confined by society, and it was normal to find a middle-aged man getting married to a girl of his daughter's age. Remarriage for a man was not banned while widow remarriages were not allowed. Widows were supposed to live a pious life and were not allowed entry in any celebration. Their presence in any good work was considered to be a bad sign. Sometimes heads of widows had their heads tonsured. Child marriage along with it brought some more problems, such as increased birth rate, poor health of women due to repeated child bearing and a high mortality rate of women and children. The use of veil or the 'purdah' system in North India was widely prevalent in the nineteenth century. It was used to protect the womenfolk from the eyes of foreign rulers who invaded India in the medieval period. But this system curtailed the freedom of women. Indian patriarchy at that time wanted to control women's sexuality by subjecting them to different ethical moral rules. It is no doubt a trauma for a girl to get herself married before she reaches puberty, and to force her into 'sex' when she is not mentally or physically prepared for a 'sexual relationship.' Thus, normal marital sexual relations for a woman had the feelings of being raped, and she was supposed to live under these inhuman conditions for the sake of some implicit false moral code.

'Gender' was a central issue for the nationalists and reformists in colonial nineteenth century India. In middle of the twentieth century, when India gained its independence, these issues occurred as a central theme in democratic constitutions. The Constitution laid down the term and idea of 'woman' disuniting from the idea of 'woman' lying with the colonial concept in people's mind.

The 86th constitutional amendment made elementary education a fundamental right for the children between the age group of 6 and 14. According to the 2001 census, the total literacy rate in India is 65.38 per cent while the female literacy rate is only 54.16 per cent.[4] The gap between rural and urban literacy rate is also very significant in India. This is evident from the fact that only 59.4 per cent of rural population is literate as compared to 80.3 per cent of the urban population, according to the 2001 census. While in 1971, only 22 per cent of Indian women were literate, by the end of 2001, 54.16 per cent female were literate. The growth of the female literacy rate is 14.9 per cent as compared to 11.7 per cent of that of male literacy rate. It is the result of many emerging 'Rebatis' in Indian social life to contribute greatly to the women's need for a free life away from the outside control of patriarchal values.

Soon after, these 'Rebatis' found themselves in the 'bread earner' status unlike their previous status of being solely dependent upon 'patriarchy' for their own existence, and they were benefited with self-determination, statehood, democracy, progress, modernity and development. Thus the total outlook on their status leads to confirm their identity and right over their own sexuality. It was not that in colonial times nobody from this mass of women raised her voice about feminine identity.

There were some writers like Toru Dutt (born: 1856) who signified the binary gender theory with an egalitarian outlook. In her *Sonnet—The Lotus*, both Cupid and Flora engage in a deliberative process, carefully weighing the merits and claims of each flower but ultimately, the poetess stresses that it is Flora, not Cupid, who decides the question. The proclamation of women's sexuality within the Indian tradition incorporates Eastern as well as Western allusions. In her poem "Savitri," included in her *Ancient Ballads and Legends of Hindustan* (1882)[5], she portrays Savitri as a free woman. It is true that Toru Dutt was not the suitable person to represent Indian poetess of that time as most of her time she used to remain in Europe. Her parents shifted to Europe when she was a mere child of 13 years. Her parents were more inclined to Western culture and she continued her writings in French and English.

In later periods, many such 'Rebatis' emerged in Indian literature and contributed greatly to the women's right over their sexuality away from an outside control of patriarchal values. Ismat Chugtai (born: 1911), Amrita Pritam (born: 1919, and Kamala Das (born: 1934) were three prominent personalities in Indian literature, who were born in colonial India and used to write in post-colonial days. Their creative output added a philosophical base to the claim that sexuality is not a hidden subject, and they tried to write on the topics which patriarchal society often considered very scary, unspeakable and shameful to contemplate.

Chughtai's most famous Urdu story is "Lihaf" (The Quilt)[6] included in her short stories collection *The Quilt and Other Stories*. It is a pioneering achievement. When it was first published, she had to defend herself before the Imperial Crown Court of India. The story deals with a lesbian encounter in a Zenana (an all-women setting) in a traditional Muslim household. The protagonist in the story, a housewife, is so lonely in her husband's house that she takes a female servant as her lover. In her story "The Veil," the beautiful young bride in forbidden by Hindu tradition to remove her own veil, and is thus forced to disobey her husband. Indeed, Chughtai's stories offer insightful glances into the rebel of a female mind over a patriarchal system. She began writing in Urdu at a time when South Asian women were still sequestered and their voice suppressed.

Chugtai was born into a not-so-orthodox Muslim family where her father was a civil servant. She was the ninth of ten children (six brothers, four sisters), and since her older sisters got married while she was very young, most of her childhood was spent in the company of her brothers and according to her, this contributed greatly to the frankness in her nature and writing. Ismat was at her best when she wrote about ordinary people, especially women. The better part of her writing shows a deep and abiding preoccupation with women's issues, particularly their cultural status and their myriad roles in Indian society. By underscoring women's struggles against the oppressive institutions of her time, she brings to her fiction an understanding of the female psyche that is unique.

Another frank-speaking writer, Amrita Pritam, also deals with the politics of female sexuality and questions gendered identities in her writing with an immediate political context. Born in a schoolteacher's family in Gujranwala, Punjab, now in Pakistan, she got married at the age of sixteen and later she found it difficult to stay with a man to whom she never ever loved. She was in love with Sahir Ludhianvi, a Urdu poet, and left her husband but Sahir then had a new woman in his life and did not marry Amrita. Later, she lived the last forty years of her life with the renowned artist and writer, Imroz. Amrita's life was like an open book and she neither wanted to hide anything nor did she deny anything in her writings. Her own life made her beliefs strong, and she used her poems and fiction to depict the sexual politics played against woman by society of that time. Whatever she experienced, she recorded in her poems and novels—her legendary love for Sahir Ludhianv or for Imroz. So many of her anecdotes revolved around her love of these two men. Once her son came to her and said, "People say that I am Sahir Uncle's son." Imagine the inner courage and conviction of a woman who could reply, "I wish you were Sahir Uncle's son."[7] Though writing in Punjabi, Amrita Pritam could represent the voices of South Asian women regarding love and sexual politics.

Another bilingual writer who could make her voice prominent to protest patriarchal values and established her will to proclaim sexual politics over female body was Kamala Das. She had a natural flair for both Malayalam and English. She was born in a conservative Hindu Nair (Nallappattu) family having royal ancestry. Her father was a former managing editor of the widely-circulated Malayalam daily *Mathrubhumi*, and her mother, Nalappatt Balamani Amma, was a renowned Malayali poetess. Her formal education stopped at the age of 15 when she was married to K. Madhava Das. She was 16 when her first son was born and she said once, "I was mature enough to be a mother only when my third child was born." Because of the great age difference between Kamala and her husband, Mr. Das often played a fatherly role for both Kamala and their sons. Her husband often encouraged her to associate with people of her own age. *My Story* is considered as her outspoken autobiography and is also a source of controversy. It contains the clear picture of her multiple affairs, her strained relationship with her husband, and so many hidden facts of her life.

In an interview, she admits that her husband was the greatest supporter of her writing career, and even when controversy swirled around her sexually-charged poetry and her unabashed autobiography, *My Story*, her husband was "very proud" of her (Warrior interview). After the death of her husband, in 1999, she converted herself to Islam and married a young chap. The poetess who always wrote about Lord Krishna and imagined to be his Radha suddenly started to address Allah. Her statement "I converted my Krishna to Islam" evoked much opposition from conservative Hindus in Kerala. However, she was bold in her decisions and continues her life according to Muslim beliefs.

The sexuality of women, which was depicted in Chugtai's fiction in generalised form, became more personified with Amrita or Kamala Das's writings. In comparison with Amrita, Das more honestly extends her exploration of womanhood and love, but her poetess self can think while sleeping in her lover's arm, "What is it to the corpse if the maggots nip?"[8] (See Das's poem In "The Maggots"[8]) Indian women, however, do not discuss these experiences in reverence to social customs. Das consistently refuses to accept their silence. Feelings of longing and loss are not confined to a private misery. They are invited into the public sphere and acknowledged. Das was so daring as describe her idea in total frankness that she could tell: "(the) musk of sweat between breasts/ The warm shock of menstrual blood" should not be hidden from one's beloved.[9] The poetess argues, "A woman should stand nude before the glass with him and allow her lover to see her exactly as she is."

What would be the differences of time between old Rebati and these new Rebatis? Say merely fifty years? But the time, the tone, the outlooks, the surroundings were totally changed and created a gap between colonial and post-colonial milieus. The Rebati of Fakir Mohan did not speak a word to her lover Basudev, but only smiled once during the tuition. But the Rebati of Kamala Das could say:

> (They) Ask me, everybody, ask me
> What he sees in me, ask me why he is called a lion,
> A libertine, ask me why his hand sways like a hooded snake
> Before it clasps my pubis. Ask me why like
> A great tree, felled, he slumps against my breasts,
> And sleeps. Ask me why life is short and love is
> Shorter still, ask me what is bliss and what its price....
>
> ("The Stone Age" from Kamala Das's *The Old Playhouse and Other Poems*)[10]

But it does not mean that the tone of women's writing has changed drastically and women writers have become more frankly speaking in these fifty years. In the post-colonial period there is a tremendous increase in the number of female writers. Many female writers were trying to portray the lives, experiences and problems of feminine world. But it is pity to note that after marriage, most of these female writers either quit writing or made themselves more adjustable to male-dominated values. Unlike Chugtai, Amrita or Das, a reader can find a shyness in their voice while relating the truth and exposing their inner self. Even their weaknesses or love relations are also not expressed clearly for fear of social scandal of their character. A typical womanish shyness prevents them from writing their actual feelings towards sex and love. This is not only due to any restriction imposed by their family, but many times we find that an idea of being a good girl encourages them to hide their own feelings and experiences.

In India, 'chastity' means a lot for a woman and it is always demanded that a female should keep her 'chastity' pure and perfect. (It is another issue that nobody asks a man for the purity and perfection of his chastity.) In the case of poetry, one can hide oneself with mystic metaphor or myth, but in fiction, one has to open oneself completely, so it is difficult for a woman to write any fictions, and sincerely hide her experiences and reactions.

Personally, while writing on women's issue or writing my creative works, I found that the feminine right to sexuality became a controversial issue in the Indian male world. Once I was requested to submit a story for a special issue of an Oriya magazine. I submitted an Oriya story entitled "Gambhiri Ghara" and the editor thanked me for my cooperation. After a few days I received a phone call from someone from that editor's office, asking me to submit another story as they would not able to publish that story. The message was conveyed by an assistant and not by the editor himself. I contacted him (editor) and asked why they would not publish that story. The editor hesitated at first and then told me I should talk to Jagadish Bhai (my husband) later regarding the reason. Such an answer made me annoyed and I asked him, did he think that my husband ever had any control over my writer's entity? The answer made me disturbed and I was determined to convert the short story into a novel. The decision resulted in my novel, *The Dark Abode* (*Gambhiri Ghara* in Oriya, *Mithya Gerosthali* in Bengali, and *Irunda Kuddaram* in Malayalam).

In the eighties, one of my stories "Rape" (published in *Waiting for Manna*) was also created controversy for its obscenity, but this story does not exhibit any sexual behaviours of its characters nor so-called vulgar words. It is a story of a woman who once dreams about having sex with a very well-known private medical practitioner and she tells her husband. The husband, though he reacts in his mind, does not show any instant irritation. Later when their child swallows a small piece of glass, he takes the protagonist and her child to that doctor and at night, he asks his wife, "Did you meet your dream partner?" The words seem to the protagonist to be insulting, as if she has been raped. This simple story, to my surprise, appeared to the male readers very hard to digest. Our patriarchal society does not allow a '*sati* woman' to have sex with anyone other than her husband, even in a dream. Later, the story was translated into all Indian languages and was also published in the Harper Collins Book of Oriya short stories.

The term sexuality, especially sexuality with respect to a female, many times has raised confusion in the masculine mind. I have been asked several times, is not this a candid and a frank portrayal of the female body anti-woman? Once in answer to one of the questions of Nilangshu Agrawal I said, "I stand just as strongly for a woman's right not to have sex (of any kind) if she doesn't want to and I believe that women who make that decision deserve support and protection as well. I refuse to be a victim of some imaginary universal male sexual sadism. As a human being, I always argue about equal status for women and I refuse to believe that by denying our sexual selves, women can be equal with men."[11]

But what I oppose is patriarchal society's unfortunate decision to grant more liberation to a man than to a woman. Our current society uses a woman as an object and not as a human being. If a painter paints a nude picture of a woman, we can appreciate it as a masterpiece. We can enjoy the erotic sculpture on wall of temples showing women's nude bodies.

We can digest all these from the pen and brush of a male artist, but if Kamala Das writes, we feel disturbed thinking that society is now in danger. When Sunil Ganguly writes about his affairs with other ladies, it is cited as a literary boldness, but when Kamala Das expresses her passion, it is considered as 'perverted thought.'

How many people became sex maniacs after reading *Ulysses*? We consider *Kama Sutra* as a classic. I never think sex is not dirty play. Our Shringar literature in Sanskrit, literature of Sangam Period in Tamil, and the erotic sculptures on temple walls prove that sex is as real as hunger, thirst, slumber, birth, death wishes, and dreams. How can you blame a woman for thinking that society is spoiled for HER only?"

There is much more confusion about the 'right over woman's body.' The body does not have to always be linked with sex or more correctly, with 'sexual behaviour' or 'sexual orientation.' In our society, the 'female body' is always kept separate from that of the male. There are restrictions and limitations for 'female bodies.' Their food habits, their clothing, their movements are always separated from that of males. The discrimination is that society does not imply any restrictions or regulations on male bodies and all restrictions are implied for female bodies only. Are not these all bodily affairs?

In the times of the original 'Rebati,' not only was remarriage of widows prohibited but they were not allowed to keep long hair or to wear colourful sari. Still today, in the time of 'modern Rebatis,' women are not allowed to enter the Aiyappa temple in Kerala. Still 'modern Rebatis' suffer from dowry burning. And these are all concerned with a 'woman's body.'

Repeatedly, I have been saying what the 'modern Rebatis' want is an equality-based binary gender system. In the West, many feminists have raised their voices against this binary system. During the second wave of feminism, there was even a trend to refuse heterosexual relationships. Many feminists declared themselves either bisexual or lesbian. Simone De Beauvoir's quotation "one is not born but rather, becomes a woman" attracted the feminist anthropologists and they tried to claim that gender is a social creation, not a natural function of sex. In her essay "Woman: Myth and Reality," De Beauvoir argued that men had made women the "other" in society by putting a false aura of "mystery" around them. And she argued that men used this as an excuse not to understand women or their problems, and not to help them but to subjugate them. She argued that this stereotyping was always done in societies by the group higher in the hierarchy to the group lower in the hierarchy so that the lower group became the "other" and had a false aura of mystery around it. And she said that this also happened with other things such as race, class and religion. But she said that it was nowhere truer than with sex, in which men stereotyped women, and used it as an excuse to organise society into a patriarchy.

I fully agree that women are harmed by these persistent myths about their place in society. We need only to look at recent events in Afghanistan, Africa and the Middle East to understand how the marginalisation of any segment of society works to undermine that society as a whole. Simone also saw herself as a "gadfly." Her intention was to force readers to look at how the world (read "European Male") distorted women, Jews and non-whites. In this essay, Simone discusses the myth and reality of women. She believes the myth of women, or rather myths of women, lead to their subordination. Though certain myths were created to subjugate women, I differ from her concept of "others." Simone adopted the idea of 'others' from Hegelian theory. While giving stress to explain a woman's definition as man's 'other' or her consequent oppression, at the same time, she tackles the way in which the preceding analyses (biological, historical, psychoanalytic, etc.) contribute to the formulation of the myth of the "Eternal Feminine."

This paradigmatic myth, which incorporates multiple myths of woman under it (such as the myth of the mother, the virgin, the motherland, nature, etc.), attempts to trap woman into an impossible ideal by denying the individuality and situations of all different kinds of women. In fact, the ideal set by the Eternal Feminine sets up an impossible expectation because the various manifestations of the myth of femininity appear as contradictory and doubled. But it is also true that for their "Eternal Feminine," women are forced to relinquish their claims to transcendence and authentic subjectivity by a progressively more stringent acceptance of the "passive" and "alienated" role. It is, I think, not always due to man's "active" and "subjective" demands. They are the woman; unknowingly accept the subjugation as a part of their inner feminine characteristics.

But it is true that some of the social structures made the woman the "other" if we consider these "others" as slaves (as Hegel used the word to describe the actual position of slave) and I fully agree with Simone that only the woman can free herself by "...thinking, taking action, working, and creating on the same terms as men. Instead of seeking to disparage them, she declares herself their equal."

Once a young female writer told me that I could write frankly as my husband is liberal and cooperative. I replied that my total audience is not confined to my husband. I have my relatives, colleagues, neighbours and readers whom I have to face.

Once I had to face a staff council meeting at my college, got humiliated, and was forced to beg for an apology for writing the story 'Jallhad' (The Butcher). The story was about a rape where the victim was an infant girl, the child of a working woman. It was also a story of the harassment faced by a working woman from the masculine sphere around her. But the story was asserted as an obscene, one and a petition was begun to remove me from my job.

More than a century has passed after the first 'Rebati' and still, the modern-day 'Rebatis' still struggle for their existence in a masculine world. In the original old story, Rebati did not speak a word. But happily, the current Rebatis have regained their voices. But are their voices confined to their own core? Perhaps the actual and real 'words,' 'sentences,' 'tones,' and 'voices' are returning. Perhaps the struggle will still continue.

References

1. Fakir Mohan Senapati, *Stories, Grass Roots*, Bhubaneswar.

2. Sastri, Sivanath (1903/2001), *Ramtanu Lahiri O Tatkalin Banga Samaj* (in Bengali), New Age Publishers Pvt. Ltd. pp.112-114.
3. *Utkal Deepika*, Vol. 16, No 44, Nov. 5, 1881.
4. *Source:* Census of India - 2001 Provisional Figures.
5. Dutt, Toru, *Ancient Ballads and Legends of Hindustan,* BibiloLife, LLC, Google Book, p.1.
6. Chughtai, Ismat, Translated by Tahira Naqvi and Syeda S. Hameed, *Kali for Women,* 2004.
7. *The Sikh Review*, Volume 54, Issues 1-6ý, Kolkata: Sikh Cultural Centre, Calcutta, 2006, p. 82.
8. de Souza, Eunice (Edited), *Nine Indian Women Poets,* Delhi: Oxford University Press, 1997, p. 13.
9. de Souza, Eunice (Edited), *Nine Indian Women Poets, Delhi*: Oxford University Press, 1997, p. 15.
10. de Souza, Eunice (Edited), *Nine Indian Women Poets,* Delhi: Oxford University Press, 1997, pp. 16-17.
11. Voice of Protest against 'Universal Male Sexual Sadism': an Interview with Sarojini Sahoo by Dr. Nilanshu Kumar Agarwal, Nebula Magazine, June 2009 issue. < http://www.nobleworld.biz/images/Agarwal.pdf.>
12. Jaydeep Sarangi—In conversation with Sarojini Sahoo, Muse India,Issue 28, Nov-Dec 2009. <http://www.museindia.com/showcurrent17.asp?id =1477>

27 Scent of a Woman's Ink

(The title of this essay is borrowed from Francine Prose's essay in Harper Magazine)[1]

In patriarchal society the literature is largely male dominated: the role of women is most often to inspire rather than to create. They are labelled as women writers and are still 'considered oddities, labelled for their difference and status as an "other"—like the "male nurse" or "lady doctor". When a review of my Bengali version of novel *The Dark Abode*[2] was published in the Bangladesh daily *Pratham Alo*, the reviewer stamped me as a "Lekhika" or women writer, to which my translator Morshed Shafiul Hassan protested. But I told my translator that I would like to prefer the title women writer because I think we have to face some problems which male writers would have not.

Virginia Woolf once said that in order for a woman to be a writer she needs a room of her own with a door and a lock, and financial security. That sounds pretty good, but is it really practicable for a female writer to lock the door for writing? They have their family, their children, their household responsibilities which always rings to pull you out of that state of muse-inspired thought. The male writers are supposed to abandon everything to search for inspiration, to lock their doors from their family and to woo any women other than his family to create divinely inspired art that we gasp upon reading. But has any woman enjoyed this right in our South Asian perspective? So is the personal and writing all about our differences as a woman? I find a lot about the conflict between being a woman, being a writer, and being a parent, partly because it's difficult to do all three at once, and while I'm having a difficult time being a writer, it doen't even get me started about the other roles I might eventually want to play in life.

Kuntala Kumari Sabat (1900-1938) was remembered in Oriya literature for her mystic strain and reformative zeal in her romantic poetry. Before marriage she developed extra-marital affairs with a fatherly person Dr.Kailash Chandra Rao, and after her marriage to Krushna Prasad Das, alias Brahmachari, she shifted to Delhi. Her pre- or post-marital life were not so peaceful, and her life was dangling between love, sex, oppression and harassment by male-dominated mentality of feudal India. But we never find any sexual agony or her own saga of life in her poems rather than a coated version of mysticism in the form of Sufi ideology. Whenever the question of writings comes, women's status is denied. Women's writing is not considered a valuable one unless the book is awarded. No woman is considered as a trend-setter of total literature besides women writings. Is there no such trendsetter female writer yet? Recently I was asked in an interview for the one of the leading Oriya daily, Why in women writings, the total human problems are not discussed I answered to them whether the problems of women are not human problem?

Whenever a female writer is interviewed, she is asked about the future of female writing. She is not asked to comment about literature irrespective to gender basis, as if women are a different species from man's world, like cows or dogs. It is true that women have a different lifestyle. But is there no separate lifestyles for males? It is a wrong concept that a female should write with her limited world confined to family and her own life. I want to mention the name of Mahasweta Devi. Is she confined to her own family and her own life? I have written the novel *Swapna Khojali Mane* on poverty and *Pakhibasa* on the downtrodden tribe of Western Orissa. There are many more instances of such writings but our critics have overlooked these facts while assessing their writings. In this matter I could name Margaret Atwood, A.S. Byatt, Iris Murdoch and Doris Lessing. These women, however, will never produce the Great Novel in the eyes of critics though they have created big, grand books that tackle social forces, ideas and politics as well as the provinces of the heart for one simple reason: they are only women. In the June 1998 issue of *Harper's Magazine* Francine Prose asked a question: "Are Women 'Writers Really Inferior?" She expressed her agony for neglecting female writers by insisting that despite the sales success of middlebrow "women's fiction"—as epitomised by Oprah Winfrey's hugely successful television book club—women writers of "serious literary fiction" can't get any respect. Not, at least, from "the more cerebral book-review pages and the literary prizes."[1]

In India the status of women writers are more critical and depressing. Once in the 40's, Unnava Lakshmi Bai (Telugu) is said to have stormed out of a large literary meeting with her 'remark, "In a thousand years of Andhra literary history, couldn't you find even a single woman?" Never a woman writer's name has been considered as the pioneer in any literature. Garujada is hailed as the first "short story" writer in Telugu, rather than Bhandari Achamamba, despite conclusive evidence. In Malayali literature women writers like Lalithambika Antarjanam, Saraswathi Amma and Rajelakshmi were less represented in comparison with other writers.

In *Harper's Magazine*, Francin Prose has revived the debate by asking whether women writers are really more prone to diminutive fictions which take place mostly in interiors, about little families with little problems, and are they really more inclined toward a soft, self-absorbed emotionality or not. Actually, Prose maintains, male writers do all of that, just as women produce works that are "fiercely unsentimental, sharply observed, immensely ambitious and inclusive."

Literary critics, mostly men, ignore the dynamic vitality in women's writing and treat it as recreational and decorative. In reviewing my anthology of short stories once Jatindra Kumar Nayak, an Oriya critic, wrote: (my) stories are as "a labyrinth of the emotional lives of woman." Readers—and especially critics—are the ones who persist in seeing a fiction as inevitably coloured by its author's gender, and the male critics always think that the domestic issues, love—are of less consequence then the depth of thought produced by male writers? In short, it is a big question now, who will determine the difference in importance between a woman's inner or outer life and a man's? The answer, until recently at least, has been men. Dalit literature accepts women opposing Manu and upper caste traditions, but brands them traitors when they challenge patriarchy within the Dalit community.

Uma Parmeswaran once wrote an article on Kamala Markandeya[4], where she described that Salman Rushdie in his novels *Shame* and *The Satanic Verses* raised the issues of race riots in Britain. But before 20 years of Rushdie, Kamala Markandeya talked not only about the violence of racism but also about other diasporic realities - educational degrees that are not given accreditation, the resistance of immigrants to the expectations of the 'host' culture, chasms of communication between generations, cultural values and needless cultural baggage. But the male dominated literary criticism placed Rushdie as a pioneer of diasporic struggle.

In India, a female writer is always considered as an inferior writer in comparison to a male one. (In any office or educational centres where male and female employees work together, you can easily notice a male subordinate never wishes or says 'good morning ' to his female superior boss) The traditional readers have a tendency to find out the hidden love affairs that have been hiding beyond a fiction of a woman writer. Till now, their mind is not prepared to accept a woman as a thinker or as a philosopher, whereas in the Vedic period there were female philosophers like Madalsa, Gargi and Maitreyi.

'There were some interesting happenings with my story writing. *Gambhiri Ghara* (The Dark Abode[5]), the most controversial novel of mine, was first written in a story form and for a special issue of an Oriya periodical. Before the publication of the short story it was rejected and I was asked to submit another story in place of *The Dark Abode*. While inquiring the reason for the rejection of my story, I was told that the editor would talk to my husband. This comment of the chief editor made me irritated and I asked the chief editor whether my husband has an authority over my writer self? The patriarchy idea of the chief editor made me transform the short story to a novel.

To conclude, I want to refer to the question posed by Linda Lowen to me. Linda is a women issue guide and a renowned journalist of *New York Times* portal. She asked me in an interview[6]: "You are known for pushing the envelope, openly discussing female sexuality in your stories and novels in a way that hadn't been done before. Isn't that risky?" And my answer to Linda was:" Yes, it is risky for a woman writer to deal with these themes in an Eastern country, and for that I face much criticism. But still I believe someone has to bear this risk to accurately portray women's feelings - the intricate mental agony and complexity which a man can never feel - and these must be discussed through our fiction."

I think this is the way in which the female writers of this century should express their commitments to literature.

References

1. Prose, Francine, "Scent of a woman's ink: Are women writers really inferior?" *Harper's Magazine*, June 1998.
2. Sahoo, Sarojini. *Mithya Gerosthali*, Trans. Morshed Safiul Hassan and Dilwar Hossain, Dhaka: Anupam Prakashani, 2007.
3. Beauvoir, Simone de, *The Second Sex*, Trans. H. M. Parshley, Penguin (New Reprint Edition 1972).

4. Parameswaran, Uma, *Kamala Markandaya*, Rawat Publishers & Distributors, 2000.
5. Sahoo, Sarojini, *The Dark Abode*, Trans. Mahendra Kumar Dash, Vadodara: Indian Age Communication, 2008.
6. Lowen, Linda, "Feminism in India - Conversation with Indian Feminist Sarojini Sahoo", *About.Com Women's Issues.*

   <http://womensissues.about.com/od/feminismequalrights/a/FeminisminIndia.htm>

•